WOMEN'S PLACE IN THE KINGDOM OF GOD
(An Exposition)

By

Rayola Kelley

Hidden Manna Publications

Women's Place in the Kingdom of God

Copyright © 2006 and 2025 by Rayola Kelley
Originally copyrighted © 1993 by Rayola Kelley

ISBN: 979-8-9994555-1-2

All rights reserved. No part of this publication may be reproduced or transmitted in any form or by any means without written permission of Gentle Shepherd Ministries.

Except where otherwise indicated, all Scripture quotations in this book have been taken from the King James Version of the Bible.

Printed in the USA

Hidden Manna Publications
P.O. Box 3572
Oldtown, ID. 83822
www.gentleshepherd.com

Facebook:
https://www.facebook.com/HiddenMannaPublications/

Dedication:

I would like to dedicate
this book to saintly women
that have forged, and
continue to do so though the
the difficulties and challenges
posed by man's religion
and this world
to come into their place
with God and fulfill their
high calling in His kingdom.

Acknowledgment:

There have been many individuals such as Sarah Rick who edited this book when she edited Volume 5. I am also thankful to all those who have encouraged me along the way when it came to this controversial subject. They have always told me to be true to myself and remain true to what the Lord has put on my heart. Thank you to each and everyone of you for seeing beyond the conventional and the nominal to embrace that which is higher, excellent, and heavenly ordained.

Contents

	Introduction	9
1	Inspiration or Tradition?	13
2	A Woman Called "Adam"	21
3	Cursed or Blessed?	31
4	The Struggle Intensifies	43
5	The Truth about Marriage	51
6	Unveiling the Truth	63
7	Restraint or Persecution?	75
8	Between a Rock and a Hard Place	85
9	The Last Shall Be First	95
10	Can Women Be Entrusted?	107
11	Let My Handmaidens Go!	117
12	A Final Thought	125
	Bibliography	131

INTRODUCTION

This book has gone through various stages of development and growth to ensure a balanced perspective about women in the kingdom of God. Women who desire to serve God outside of the acceptable roles of conventional Christianity often enter a war zone that can bring them under grave scrutiny. The invisible battle they encounter has nothing to do with their call, "per se," or with their abilities, but rather, with their gender.

No doubt, there are differences between men and women. The distinction is clearly defined by physical appearance and function. Women's scriptural responsibility in the family is irrevocably outlined, but their place in the kingdom of God has been a matter of controversy through the ages.

Battling prejudice born out of cultural and religious influences has left many women frustrated and often angry. Bound by man's tradition and unrealistic standards (and, in some incidents, a few misconstrued scriptures), many women find themselves victims of their own sex.

A casual observation of most of the world's cultures verifies the fact that women are indeed victims. Treated as substandard or as mere property to use as one wills, they have often been deprived of the basics of human rights and dignity.

When considering these societies, it is interesting to note their pitiful condition. Plagued with insurmountable problems, they are crumbling from within. On the other hand, cultures that recognize the human dignity of women have flourished. Can we, therefore, conclude from this observation that the success of a society rests, at least in part, on how women are regarded?

The subject of women's place in the kingdom of heaven has haunted me. Desirous to serve God, I found myself corralled in unsatisfactory roles. These controlled roles stifled and robbed me of my need to please my Lord according to what I sensed He had put on my heart.

In my frustration, I began to seek God's perspective on women. If His perspective was in compliance with man's conventional beliefs, I was willing to deny the raging fire in my own soul and submit to such boundaries. If they did not agree, I had no choice but to consider them to be mere man's concepts or limited, prejudicial interpretations and could, therefore, reject them.

I reasoned that the kingdom of God belonged to God alone. Isaiah 55:8-9 declares God's ways are higher than man's ways. I knew in my heart the call and fire in my spirit could not be left in the hands of human reasoning.

Faithful to His Word, God answered my prayers. He revealed priceless information to me over the years. My findings not only upheld the fire in my spirit, but also set me free to pursue a life of service beyond normally acceptable boundaries.

My prayer is that these findings will set others free. God's perspective must replace the ideology man has often conveniently hidden behind as a cover for what seems as cultural conditioning, ignorance, insecurity, and/or pride on their part. The liberty of the Spirit must reign where prejudice formerly dictated. Truth must overcome ignorance and Satan's lies. God must truly become Lord in those areas where man has unscripturally exalted his own authority and personal interpretation.

No one will deny God has established sound rules for the home. However, the Bible is also clear regarding orderly and godly conduct as a requirement for both sexes. In the kingdom of God, Jesus is LORD! He determines the position each servant is to have in His work. His decision will not be based on sex. Galatians 3:26-28 states,

> For ye are <u>all</u> the children of God by faith in Christ Jesus. For as many of you as have been baptized into Christ have put on Christ. There is neither Jew nor Greek, there is neither bond nor free, there is neither <u>male</u> nor <u>female</u>; for ye are all one in Christ Jesus. (Emphasis added.)

1

INSPIRATION OR TRADITION?

Based on 2 Timothy 3:16, few Christians will question the validity of the Bible. This scripture states, "All scripture is given by inspiration of God, and is profitable for doctrine, for reproof, for correction, for instruction in righteousness." Clearly, the Word is meant to bring forth correction in how we think, act, and conduct the affairs of our lives. It is to bring us to a place of right standing before God and upright or honorable conduct towards others. The purpose for this instruction in righteousness is to bring perfection or maturity in our lives that will express itself in good works.[1]

The author of the Word of God is the Holy Spirit. Since the Holy Spirit is behind the inspiration, integrity, and validity of the Word, we must conclude that it is not just a book with various statements that is meant to only reach the intellect. Rather, it is a book that can only be discerned and understood from the basis of spirit. Jesus stated that His words are spirit and life.[2] Therefore, only the Holy

---
[1] John 6:63; 2 Timothy 3:17
[2] 2 Peter 1:20-21

Spirit can bring the proper perspective to spiritual matters, producing the life that will speak of righteousness. The Apostle Paul verified this fact in 1 Corinthians 2:13-14,

> Which things also we speak, not in the words which man's wisdom teacheth, but which the Holy Ghost teacheth; comparing spiritual things with spiritual. But the natural man receiveth not the things of the Spirit of God; for they are foolishness unto him: neither can he know them, because they are spiritually discerned.

During my years of ministry, I discovered that Christians have one of three perceptions by which they evaluate scriptural principles. These perceptions are based on Spirit and truth, or a literal perception, or from the stance of religion with its traditions.

These perceptions vary in approach, attitude, and action towards the Word of God. For example, the perception that is based on Spirit and truth is a perspective that desires to line up with God's heart (intent) and thoughts toward a matter. The Holy Spirit becomes the teacher who will be allowed to convict of sin and to reprove believers as to what is righteousness and what will serve as judgment. His ultimate goal is to lead each of us to the truth of Jesus Christ and His teachings.[3]

The Holy Spirit will establish us on the foundation of Jesus Christ. This means He will compare spiritual things with spiritual things as precept is carefully placed upon

---

[3] John 16:7-15; 1 John 2:27

precept (doctrine), and lines of truth upon lines of truth.[4] As the foundation is established, it will unveil Jesus Christ to us, in us, and through us.

As we allow the Holy Spirit to use the Word in the right manner, the Word becomes a sharp sword that will penetrate the soul and spirit, exposing our motives, dispositions, and attitudes. Such a dividing is able to produce humility, meekness, and submission. It will bring liberty to the soul, allowing us the freedom to discover God and to move forward in service and worship before Him.[5]

Clearly, if the Holy Spirit is missing, the Word of God will never make an impact on our lives. It will be lifeless and maintained on an intellectual level that will keep us indifferent to the heart of God and the reality around us.

This brings us to the other two approaches. The literalist approach to the Bible is to accept the letter of the Scripture. This may seem appropriate, but there is one problem with this approach—it will lack spirit. It will fail to consider matters in light of the spiritual aspect. Therefore, discerning the intent of Scripture in light of the complete Word of God will be absent.

The Word of God speaks of the mystery that is hidden in Scripture. This mystery was unveiled, but there is great depth to the mystery that the carnal finite mind will fail to see unless the Holy Spirit reveals it. To lack the right spirit in approaching the Bible will cause understanding to

---

[4] Isaiah 28:10, 13; 1 Corinthians 3:11
[5] John 4:24; 8:32; 2 Corinthians 3:17; Hebrews 4:12

become dead-letter, or, in other words, it will lack the life to impact the soul and spirit of man.[6]

Any perception based on religion or tradition also has the opposite effect in a person's life. Jesus declared that such an approach actually nullifies the Word of God. A person who operates from this perspective will try to adjust the Word to their beliefs or practices, rather than allow the Word to line them up to the nature and will of their Holy God. Thus, the Word is rendered powerless to change the lives of these types of individuals.

This is a dangerous practice. Jesus advocated that religious practices may give the appearance of righteousness, but the inward man lacks life. He described such individuals as white sepulchers that appear beautiful on the outside, but, from within, are full of dead men's bones and uncleanness.[7]

To adjust the Word of God to personal beliefs is the same as adjusting the narrow path that leads to life, making it more acceptable as one merrily goes on their way to hell.[8] Sadly, it is a natural tendency of man's religion to adjust the narrow path established by Jesus, while submitting to a religious lifestyle that displays an outward righteousness, but is devoid of a right heart attitude. Jesus made mention of this heart condition.

He said that even though some religious people honored Him with their lips, their hearts were far from Him. Matthew 15:8 identifies the source behind traditions as

---

[6] Romans 7:6; 2 Corinthians 3:2-3, 6; Ephesians 3:3-5; Colossians 2:2-3
[7] Matthew 15:6; 23:27
[8] Matthew 7:13-14

belonging to man and not inspired by the Holy Spirit. The result of tradition is bondage and death. We read this declaration from Jesus in Matthew 23:13 and 15,

> But woe unto you, scribes and Pharisees, hypocrites! for ye shut up the kingdom of heaven against men: for ye neither go in yourselves, neither suffer ye them that are entering to go in…Woe unto you, scribes and Pharisees, hypocrites! for ye compass sea and land to make one proselyte, and when he is made, ye make him twofold more the child of hell than yourself.

These religious people used the Word of God for their own purposes. They made it ineffective with their own interpretations, resulting in death. This is why the Apostle Paul made this reference in 2 Corinthians 3:6, "Who also hath made us able ministers of the new testament; not of the letter, but of the spirit: for the letter killeth, but the spirit giveth life."

Jesus came to set us free, not to enslave us with more rules. His light burden is to love Him, and His easy yoke is to learn of Him.[9] Obviously, it is important that we consider our perception.

As Christians, it is our responsibility to handle the Word correctly in all spiritual matters. This would include the subject of women's place in the kingdom of God. We must approach a matter in the right spirit in order to end with truth that ensures the integrity of God's character and the

---
[9] Matthew 11:28-20

pure intent of His Word. It is such an approach that will allow the Word of God to have its way in our lives.

I have learned that I must hold my opinions lightly and be quick to discard every belief that does not maintain spirit and truth. I am obligated to test all of my beliefs to determine whether they bring me liberty in the spirit, or bondage as a result of man-made rules.

This study about women may challenge your perception. Remember, challenges are positive as long as you do as the Bereans did in Acts 17:11. They were eager to receive the message of truth, but they also examined it to see if it was true or consistent with what they already knew to be true. After all, there are no inconsistencies in God's truth.

Obviously, the real issue is not whether something agrees with a particular way of thinking, but whether it agrees with God. As I have confronted this issue of women's place in God's kingdom, I have discovered that people who stumble over this issue err in one of three ways: 1) they are either erring in how they handle the Word of God due to their approach; 2) they are erring due to ignorance about the cultural, religious, and political influences of that day; and/or 3) they are erring in their knowledge and attitude about the character of God.

My hope is that reader will examine this information in light of the complete Word of God to ensure its spirit and integrity. I pray they will allow the Holy Spirit to form their conclusions, rather than traditional religious beliefs that are often literal in their interpretation. I hope each person will see my goal in writing this book is to help anyone who might be in bondage concerning this particular issue.

As you read this material, open your heart and mind to the Holy Spirit. Give Him permission to help you explore this controversial subject in a way that will be both pleasing to Him and liberating for you!

2

A WOMAN CALLED "ADAM"

A very important question to ask about women is why did God create Eve? The old standby answer comes from Genesis 2:18, "And the LORD God said, It is not good that the man should be alone; I will make him an help mate for him."

We know that God brought every creature to Adam to name. However, according to Genesis 2:20, there was no real suitable helper to be found in all of creation for the man.

The general consensus is that woman was formed from the side of man to serve as his helper. This belief has given way to attitudes marking women with a stigma of inferiority and servitude. But, is this a correct attitude?

In his viewpoint about the term "helper", Skip Moen pointed out that God did not refer to Eve as woman, wife, or female. It was Adam who first called her "woman" because she was taken out of his side.[1] According to Moen, the word "helper" comes from the Hebrew word "ezer," which points to masculine gender. He also pointed

---
[1] Genesis 2:22

out it is the same word or noun that is used to describe God's relationship to Israel. In other words, God is the helper (protector and provider) of His chosen people.

Moen points out other uses of the word "helper" in the Bible that give the sense of "save from danger," "deliver from death," and "succor". Clearly, this word carries the concept of someone who has superior strength in the matter of being a helper, provider, and protector, rather than one who is inferior.

By using this term, God is clearly establishing the fact that woman was not created from the standpoint of being inferior, but equal. Why should this surprise us? After all, if woman was taken out of man, one could only reason that she is of the same quality and caliber as Adam and is, therefore, equal to him.

What or who reduced women to a substandard or inferior state? Obviously, God did not put woman in such a light. In fact, He initially foreshadowed, in the garden, the reality that it was through woman the Messiah would come to save and deliver those who believe. There can only be one explanation of why women have been displaced into an inferior position and existence. It must be due to the effect of sin working within the human heart and mind.

We must gain God's perspective to see if woman is capable of being the "helper," equal in every way that God intended her to be. To understand it in a proper perspective, it is important that we consider all of scripture concerning the creation of man.

Genesis 5:1b-2 states, "In the day that God created man, in the likeness of God made he him; Male and female created he them; and blessed them, and called their name Adam, in the day when they were created." Keep in mind that woman was in Adam when he was formed from the dust of the earth. God already acknowledged that He had created both of them. When God created man, He made <u>them</u> in His likeness. He called them both "Adam" or "man," which means red, signifying the earth. This shows God made no distinction between man and woman, displaying equality in importance and purpose.

We know woman was fashioned from the side of Adam.[2] One cannot help but note Christ's words on this subject in relationship to the sanctity of marriage in Matthew 19:4-5, "And he answered and said unto them, Have ye not read, that he which made them at the beginning made them male and female. And said, For this cause shall a man leave father and mother, and shall cleave to his wife: and they twain shall be one flesh?" In light of this consideration, we can possibly see how marriage would be symbolic of restoring man back to his original state. But, all of this speculation still brings us back to a woman called "Adam."

Can we assume the conventional belief surrounding the forming of woman was simply based on Adam's need for a helper? Is there more to the story? Keep in mind that "helper" pointed to one who was equal and had the strength to provide what was necessary, as well as protect.

---

[2] Genesis 2:21-22

But, in what way would woman serve as such a helper? To examine this issue further, we need to consider the fall of man.

The popular approach of the Church has been to focus on the woman. After all, she was the one deceived by the master of deception. She confessed to this truth in Genesis 3:13. Although many have falsely accused Eve of lying about being deceived, the Apostle Paul concurred with her in the New Testament in 2 Corinthians 11:3 and 2 Timothy 2:14.

In 2 Corinthians 11:3, the Apostle Paul stated that the serpent beguiled Eve. "Beguiled" in this text means to seduce wholly.[3] In 1 Timothy 2:14, Paul told us that woman was in transgression because of this deception. Clearly, Eve had no intention of being deceived and giving in to Satan's temptation in the garden.

The normal procedure is to point the finger of mockery at the woman's vulnerability to Satan's lies. This mockery could be justified if Satan's ability to deceive was limited to women alone. But, as we see in 2 Corinthians 11:3, Paul was concerned about men falling for Satan's lies as well.

Those who point their fingers at the obvious manage to ignore the true cause behind man's fall. Paul told us in 1 Timothy 2:14 that Adam <u>was not deceived</u>, therefore Adam deliberately sinned. Job 31:33 gives us this special insight about Adam's condition, "If I covered my transgressions as Adam, by hiding mine iniquity in my bosom."

---

[3] Strong's Exhaustive Concordance of the Bible, #1818

Adam had transgression hidden in his heart. In other words, he was already considering transgressing the covenant that God had made with him. Such an attitude is considered treachery. What was the covenant? It was not to eat of the tree of knowledge of good and evil.[4]

Clearly, something was amiss in Adam's character. His spiritual condition was revealed even more when he blamed not only woman for his disobedient decision, but God as well! It was, after all, God who gave him a woman. We read Adam's accusation in Genesis 3:12, "And the man said, The woman whom <u>thou</u> gavest to be with me, she gave me of the tree, and I did eat." (Emphasis added.)

For Adam to blame a holy, perfect God for his <u>own</u> sinful action should serve as a powerful clue to Adam's inward spiritual condition. This brings us to the real truth about fallen man ascribed in Romans 5:12, "Wherefore, as by one man sin entered into the world, and death by sin; and so death passed upon all men, for that all have sinned."

Sin and its consequence came through Adam and <u>not Eve</u>! Sin existed in Adam's heart before he even fell in the garden. The proof of this is evidenced in his attitude towards God's provision and command.

We know that, after God had finished creating man on the sixth day, he looked upon his creation and considered that "it was very good" (Genesis 1:31b).

In Genesis 2:18, we see a change from God's first declaration of "it was very good" to "it is not good." What happened between the sixth day of creation and God's

---

[4] Genesis 2:16-17; Hosea 6:7

declaration in Genesis 2:18? Adam had it all. He was complete as part of God's creation and had fellowship with God. He lived in Paradise.

The first clue there was a problem is seen in Adam's disregard for God's provision. In Genesis 2:16-17, we are given this insight. God commanded Adam to freely eat from any tree in the garden, except the tree of the knowledge of good and evil

We know from Genesis 2:9 that one of the trees Adam could have eaten from was the tree of life. But, according to Genesis 3:22, Adam did not eat of the tree of life. This verse reads, "And the LORD God said, Behold, the man is become as one of us, to know good and evil: and now, lest he put forth his hand, and take also of the tree of life, and eat, and live for ever"

Adam could have chosen life, but instead he chose death. Adam also showed disregard for his responsibility in the garden. In Genesis 1:26, we see how God gave man rule over His creation. In Genesis 2:15, we read that his responsibility in the garden was to dress and keep it.

The word "dress" implies work that is done from the basis of servitude, while "keep" means to put a hedge about, protect, guard, attend to, preserve, regard, serve, and watch.[5] Since there were no thistles, sweat, or struggle with the ground until after the fall, what did Adam have to oversee?

Perhaps his work had to do with protecting his domain from Satan, guarding his relationship with his Creator,

---

[5] Strong's Exhaustive Concordance of the Bible; # 5647 & 8104

attending to the matters of the heart, preserving the perfect environment, regarding the covenant with his God, serving in humility, and watching over the complete welfare of the garden.

Keep in mind that Adam had rule over the garden. He had an obligation to keep it. If he was dedicated to God, devoted to his wife, and responsible towards what had been entrusted to him, why did he allow the presence of Satan to intrude into this perfect paradise?

Some Bible scholars feel the real meaning behind Adam "being alone" in Genesis 2:18 actually implies there was a separation occurring between Adam and his God. Adam was created in the image of God. He lived in a perfect environment. How could this perfect picture change unless Adam began to change in his attitude towards his Creator?

Based upon these conclusions, some Bible scholars believe God formed woman for the sole purpose of pointing Adam back to Himself. In Professor Katharine C. Bushnell's studies on this subject, she noted that the late Dr. Alexander Whyte, in his book *Bible Characters*, maintained this concept. He wrote, "There must have been something of the nature of a stumble, if not an actual fall, in Adam while yet alone in Eden . . . Eve was created to 'help' Adam to recover himself, and to establish himself in Paradise, and in the favor, fellowship and service of his Maker."

Bushnell also pointed out that other respected Bible scholars of her time (1923) were in agreement with these conclusions, but they were being ignored by the generality of Bible expositors.[6]

The idea that a woman called "Adam" was formed to point man back to God as a means to confront or protect him from giving way to moral deviation that was present in his character is indeed a challenge to traditional views. The general approach to this subject has left woman scorned, and deprived of any mercy or forgiveness. She has been left "holding the bag" for not only man's initial fall, but also his succession of sins. However, the question we must seriously ask ourselves is who has failed whom?

Scripture clearly reveals Adam's failure, not only to his Creator and the Creation, but also to woman. One must ask, why was woman deceived in the first place? Deception comes out of ignorance of God. This ignorance could have only existed because the man who walked with God did not take the responsibility to lead his wife into an intimate understanding or fellowship with her Creator.

On this note I will leave the reader to ponder these inspiring and challenging thoughts by W.L. Heslop,

> Adam was first formed, and then Eve. She was taken out of man and built for the man as a helper, guide, philosopher, and friend. As the last created, the woman was the best and most honored of all. She was not made directly from the dust of the ground, but built from a living, warm portion of man's body. Man was created from the cold, soulless dust. The woman was one step farther

---

[6] God's Word To Women; study note 32

removed from the earth than the man, and was intended to pull man upward and heavenward. *(Seed Thoughts)*

3

CURSED OR BLESSED?

During the ERA movement in the 1970s, a well-known TV preacher blamed woman's dissension on their husbands. At the time, I felt it quite noble for him to elude that men might have played an invisible role in this movement.

Attitudes from both the secular and Church world have helped fuel the fire of this movement. Although the ERA movement is motivated by a sinister plan to destroy the family and this nation and usher in Communistic, humanistic ideology, it would serve each of us well if we would consider the prevalent attitudes surrounding women. Obviously, the problem does not solely rest on the shoulders of one particular gender, but with the blatant reality that attitudes towards gender are often conditioned according to cultural and religious influences.

Unhappy women, who are unaware of the underlying goal of ERA, have joined their ranks to vent suppressed anger and frustration. Striving to maintain some measure of dignity, respect, consideration, and control over their lives, these ladies have become mere puppets to a movement that will sacrifice them in the end.

The question is how can we change this movement? I have already alluded to the problem. The answer is simple; it begins with changing attitudes. Because of one wrong action in the Garden, women have been plagued for centuries by stories making them accursed. Pagan tales such as Pandora's Box have sent subliminal messages promoting attitudes which make women scapegoats for every ailment of society.

What about the Church? Are attitudes towards women inspired by pagan and unfounded beliefs? Those in the Church who harbor wrong attitudes would answer with a resounding "No!" They would then back their answer with a few scriptures, taken out of context, to justify both their unscriptural, unloving attitudes and actions.

Let us now begin to examine our attitudes in light of the Word of God. Many misconceptions have been established by the types of emphasis church leaders have put on the fall of man. When we think of the fall, we automatically focus on Eve being deceived. According to popular belief, because she was deceived, she received a curse from God, which she and those of her gender must forever endure. To guarantee she pays for leading Adam down the wrong path, she, along with all other females, must gracefully bear this curse of being regarded and treated as substandard, foolish, and insignificant. After all, isn't it their deserved lot in life?

Consider that sin and death came through <u>one</u> man. The Apostle Paul mentioned this fact eight times. He identified the culprit to be Adam in two of these scriptures.[1]

We know Eve was truly deceived, but Adam was not. According to Job 31:33, Adam had sin hidden in his heart. We know from the Genesis account that, instead of owing up to his actions, he blamed both Eve and God. Was it Adam or Eve who rebelled against God?

Let's just assume for a moment that women <u>are</u> cursed. Does this idea that all women must pay in some way really line up to the complete counsel of God? Ezekiel 18:19-20 gives us this insight,

> Yet say ye, Why? Doth not the son bear the iniquity of the father? When the son hath done that which is lawful and right, and hath kept all my statutes, and hath done them, he shall surely live. The soul that sinneth, it shall die. The son shall not bear the iniquity of the father, neither shall the father bear the iniquity of the son; the righteousness of the righteous shall be upon him, and the wickedness of the wicked shall be upon him.

Has God changed? Are women to be held accountable for Eve's response in the garden or for their own actions? Galatians 3:13 gives this decisive blow to the concept that women are under a curse, "Christ hath redeemed us from the curse of the law, being made a curse for us; for it is written, Cursed is everyone that hangeth on a tree."

---

[1] See Romans 5:14-19; 1 Corinthians 15:22; 1 Timothy 2:14

Christ brings liberty from the curse, not bondage. Those who believe upon Him are no longer under a curse. We must ask why are there those in the Church who insist on putting women under some curse in the name of Christ? What are they really hiding?

It is amazing to me that Christian men and women would stand behind this idea. Basically, what this perception says is that woman's lot as a wife is a matter of a curse and not a privilege. If this is true, why marry? One must also ask, where does the dignity of the husband rest when their wife's submission is solely motivated and maintained by a curse, and not because of love and commitment? Where is the sweet victory?

According to Katharine C. Bushnell, the Babylonian Talmud inspired some of the church's belief and attitude.[2] These writings are not a translation of scripture, but a collection of Jewish traditions. They came from what was known as the Oral Law of the Jews.

This law was not written down until 100 AD.[3] However, it stood as law for how women were to conduct themselves. The Talmud actually pronounced ten curses on women. These ten curses have demoted women from the status of a human being to a depraved object that has no rights because of Eve's action.

I realize some Christians are armed with their "pat" scriptures to justify their beliefs. One such scripture is

---

[2] God's Word To Women, study notes 102-106 & 132
[3] Difficult Sayings (article)

found in Genesis 3:16. Some uphold that God pronounced a curse on Eve, but did He? Let us examine this incident.

Eve was deceived. She did not evade this truth. She simply confessed it to God.[4] In Genesis 3:14, we see God putting the blame on the serpent for deceiving her and pronouncing a curse on the creature, "And the LORD God said unto the serpent, Because thou hast done this, thou art cursed above all cattle, and above every beast of the field; upon thy belly shalt thou go, and dust shalt thou eat all the days of my life."

In Genesis 3:17-19, we see God declaring the consequences Adam must face because of his rebellion. However, in close proximity of these two declarations (verses 17 and 19), we see Him saying this to the serpent about Eve in Genesis 3:15, "And I will put enmity between thee and the woman, and between thy seed and her seed; he shall bruise thy head, and thou shalt bruise his heel."

In Romans 16:20, we see Paul identifying Satan as the one who will be crushed, "And the God of peace shall bruise Satan under your feet shortly. The grace of our Lord Jesus Christ be with you. Amen."

We see God bringing a separation between Eve and Satan. Remember, it was Satan who used the serpent to deceive. We must note that we do not see this enmity being put between Adam and Satan.

Hebrews 2:14 tells us that Jesus Christ was the promise mentioned in Genesis 3:15 that would bring victory, "Forasmuch, then, as the children are partakers of flesh

---

[4] Genesis 3:13

and blood, he also himself likewise took part of the same, that through death he might destroy him that had the power of death, that is, the devil."

We know that the offspring mentioned in Genesis 3:15 are those who are born of the spirit. In John 1:12-13, we read this promise, "But as many as received him, to them gave he power to become the sons of God, even to them that believe on his name; Who were born, not of blood, nor of the will of the flesh, nor of the will of man, but of God."

Consider how this spiritual birth has nothing to do with the plan or decision of man, nor will it be the result of a husband's attempt. This birth will come out of the will of God and it will be executed through a woman.

In fact, the promise of the coming Messiah was very real among the young maidens of the Orthodox Jewish Belief. It was the longing of all believing Jewish handmaidens to be the mother of the Messiah.

In Genesis 3:15, we see God bestowing the greatest promise on Eve. The question we must consider is why would God pronounce a blessing on Eve and then turn around and curse her? In Bushnell's book *God's Word to Women*, she explained how the curse was a product of Satan and not a consequence determined by God.

Satan hated the woman. Remember that God had put enmity between her and him. God gave a promise of redemption that would come through woman. By revealing the original meaning of the Hebrew translation of this scripture, Bushnell uncovered a mistranslation that has served to carry out the very hatred Satan has towards the vessel God would one day use to bring about His plan of redemption.

This hatred would put woman under bondage. It would encourage hatred in the one closest to her who would have the responsibility to love her as his own body.

Let us look at this deviation in translation that Bushnell exposed with her expertise of the Hebrew language. For history's sake, she posed that the original translation was lost with an earlier Greek version that came into being around 175 A.D. Instead of the following translation, "Unto the woman he said, I will greatly multiply thy sorrow and thy conception; in sorrow thou shalt bring forth children", Bushnell cited this to be the correct translation taken from the Septuagint, "Unto the woman He said, "A snare has increased your sorrow and your sighing . . ."[5]

The snare is Satan who waits to bring sorrow upon women of all ages. This sorrow becomes evident as women in every generation watch their children suffer, not only due to the travail of birth, but to the hardness of those who travel the way of transgression, as well as Satan's destruction of their spiritual well-being. We can even see a prophetical culmination of this truth in the life of Mary, the mother of Jesus.

Mary had considered herself blessed to be entrusted with the Messiah, but then came the sorrow as she stood at the foot of His cross.[6] The prophet Simeon described her future sorrow with these words in Luke 2:35, "Yea, a

---

[5] God's Word To Women; study notes 117-120
[6] John 19:25

sword shall pierce through thy soul also, that the thoughts of many hearts may be revealed."

Think about how broken Mary's heart must have been. She witnessed the incredible price of Adam's disobedience, as well as the reality of Satan's hatred and goal to destroy souls for eternity.

There has been confusion over the second part of Genesis 3:16 concerning a woman's rights and place in the Church. It has served as a frame of reference for the interpretation of other scriptures pertaining to women. For this reason, Bushnell referred back to various versions in her book, including the Septuagint, to establish the correct translation. Instead of this translation, "…and thy desire shall be to thy husband, and he shall rule over thee," the correct translation should be rendered: "You are turning away (from Me) to your husband, and he will rule over you."[7]

An Italian Dominican monk by the name of Pagnino replaced the word "turning" with the word "desire." In this context, the word "desire" means lust.[8] According to Pagnino's take on this text, the woman's lust would totally hinge on her husband. Lust is totally associated with the works of the flesh.[9] According to James 1:14-15, such lust ends in death.

When we consider this concept, we see it is not realistic. A woman would have to be a robot to adhere to this perception, for she would have to lose her personality and

---

[7] God's Word To Women; study notes 124-126, 130-137
[8] Ibid, study notes 141-144
[9] Galatians 5:16-21

individuality and cease to feel or think. She would end up serving the whims of her husband's appetites and demands, regardless of the spiritual implications of a matter. This would make her a slave to something that could easily prove to be sinister and ungodly. In fact, her husband would serve as her god or lord, which is scripturally unacceptable.

As the Bible has pointed out, people can only serve one master at a time, and there is only one God and one Lord. Obviously, man in his fallen state of sin is unable to fill such a billing, even in the capacity of a husband.[10]

The Apostle Peter settled the issue of who women must obey in Acts 5:29b, "We ought to obey God rather than men."

In 1 Corinthians 6:20, the Apostle Paul stated we were bought with a price; therefore, we should glorify God in our bodies and spirits. He goes on to say in 1 Corinthians 7:23 that, since we are bought with a price, we must not be servants of men. Clearly, as believers we are not here to serve mere man, but the living God who redeemed us with the blood of His Son.

By honestly studying the Word of God, we can safely conclude that the translation that stands consistent in light of other scriptures is the word "turning." In Genesis 3:16, God was actually telling Eve that, since she was turning away from Him to be with Adam, she would come under the rule of her husband. Sadly, the rule of men is often according to their selfish, arrogant dispositions. Rather

---

[10] Isaiah 43:10-11; Matthew 6:24; Ephesians 4:4-6; 1 Corinthians 8:5-6

than serving as the example of Christ's meek leadership, they come across as tyrannical dictators that simply see their wives as substandard and a possession.

Many have made Adam look noble by stating that it was Adam's love for Eve that inspired his treachery against God's covenant. It is time to set the record straight as to who gave up what.

If Adam loved Eve, why didn't he lead her away from the serpent and his temptation? After all, Genesis 3:6 states he was <u>with</u> her during the temptation. If he loved Eve, why didn't he lead her <u>away</u> from the tree of knowledge <u>to</u> the tree of life? True love desires to protect.

God expelled <u>the man</u> Adam from the garden, lest he would eat of the tree of life.[11] Granted, the term "man" could apply to both Adam and Eve. However, it is interesting to note that the LORD God sent him forth from the garden. If Bushnell is correct about the translation of Genesis 3:16b, the woman had a choice to remain under God's rule or follow Adam. Inevitably, God already knew she would choose to follow Adam.

If this is true, there is nowhere in scripture where we can find that God actually expelled Eve. She simply followed Adam. She left the garden and the protective rule of her Creator. If this is so, because of Eve's choice to follow Adam, many women have tasted the cruelty of man's rule through the ages.

Is woman cursed or blessed? Let me answer the question according to my perception of the information that

---

[11] Genesis 3:22-24

we have been considering. Because Eve was blessed by God, she became cursed by Satan. This curse has made her a target and a victim by those who have never allowed themselves to be separated from the darkness of their own hearts and from the god of this world.

Women, the only way you can cease to be a victim is to reverse Eve's decision. Come back and submit yourself under the protective hand of your loving Creator. He has a garden prepared for each of you. This garden overflows with love, joy, peace, mercy, grace, purity, and liberty. Above all else, know that your eternal bridegroom, Jesus Christ, is waiting for you with open arms.

4

THE STRUGGLE INTENSIFIES

One of my struggles with the issue of women in God's kingdom has been how it has been presented in the Word of God. For all of my Christian life, I have believed that all Scriptures have been inspired just as the Word declares.[1] Clearly, any literalist would conclude from the few Scriptures that make reference to women that they are to be strictly seen and not heard.

To conclude that a few Scriptures might be improperly handled would appear to put serious doubt on the rest of the Word of God. As a woman, I struggled with this very issue. If a person took liberty with Genesis 3:16, then how many other men have taken liberty with the rest of the Word of God?

My struggle to uphold the integrity of the Word of God was intense enough that I was almost willing to let the issue of women slide. On the other hand, was I willing to

---

[1] 2 Timothy 3:16

sacrifice my life in God to keep a façade of calmness? Is the Word of God so weak that it cannot be challenged?

As I studied the character of God, I realize that the truth will stand any challenge. However, truth had to be defined. Such definition would come down to the God of the Bible. All truth would line up to His character. It would be consistent to His Spirit and ways. As I studied deliverance, I realized God's truth does not put people in bondage; rather, it brings liberty to them.[2]

Since truth will stand in the midst of all challenges, all discrepancies or places of confusion in God's Word must be honestly challenged. As I considered the complete Word of God, I had no doubt all Scriptures have been inspired, but that does not mean man has not occasionally taken liberty with them. But such inconsistencies will be discovered when compared with the complete Word of God.

Another matter that I am sure of is that the intent of the Word has always been maintained. If you consider the sure Word of God, it comes down to prophecy.[3] In other words, we can be sure of the validity of the Word of God because of prophecy, not because of technicality. Even in the Gospels, there are what some consider discrepancies when, in fact, they represent different eye-witness presentations of something. For example, not every witness sees or hears the same thing. However, when you study the different incidents in the Gospels, you will clearly

---

[2] John 8:32-36; 14:6; 2 Corinthians 13:8
[3] 2 Peter 1:20-21

see the consistency of the spirit or intent behind each incident.

This brings me to the matter of spirit. In spite of the few discrepancies, I have encountered in my studies of God's Word, if a person approaches a matter in the right spirit, the so-called "discrepancies" will not change a person's perception, attitude, or conduct. In other words, if a man is righteous, the few Scriptures that appear to disparage women will not change the righteous ways of how he already looks, regards, or treats women. Questionable Scriptures will only advance those who are hiding behind indoctrination, prejudices, personal agendas, and ignorance.

Hence, enter the discrepancies. It is important to consider in what ways the various translators throughout the years might possibly take liberty with Scripture. Could they honestly take liberty with God's character, Law, history, or dealings with man? The answer is not really.

God's character is clearly seen throughout His Word, His Law is indelibly established, His dealings with man are a matter of record, and history has its own checks and balances. For example, you could not change King David's sins of adultery and murder without throwing out Psalm 51. The history of the kings was also a matter of record.

However, the places in which man could take liberty with the Word would be at points of semantics, instructions, cultural influences, and customs. For example, the word "man" in Scripture does not necessary mean just men, but can be an indefinite pronoun that can embrace the concept of someone, anyone, or a certain one. For example, in Matthew 16:24 where Jesus stated if any man will come after me, "man" in this text means anyone.[4]

Obviously, the call to preach the Gospel and make disciples is not just extended to men, but to women as well. This means women must preach and teach. Therefore, the term "men" in such Scripture as 2 Timothy 2:2 where it talks about faithful men who are competent to teach others can be a generic term for mankind or a human being.[5]

Another term that can include women is the "position of a bishop." This term is actually the feminine word "episcope". The position of bishop was the same as the elder. In Titus 2:3-4, elder women were instructed to teach and admonish the younger women. Obviously, this required the elder women to take authority over others, but, apparently, it was not just restricted to instructing women about their conduct in the matters of life. The qualities established for both elder women and men in 1 Timothy 3:2-3 and Titus 1:8-9 sound like the same qualities that were established for those in the office of elders.[6]

Phoebe was a deacon. Although the word "deacon" was translated as minister and servant when referring to her, she was a powerful influence in the early Church.[7] According to historical information, she was widely traveled and had a legal mind. She argued cases for the

---

[4] Difficult Sayings (article)
[5] Ibid
[6] Ibid
[7] Romans 16:1

churches in the courts of her land. She was an evangelist and superintendent of at least two churches.[8] Clearly, the Apostle Paul recognized her leadership because he told those at the Roman Church in Romans 16:1 to give her any help she may need from them.

Obviously, by changing the meaning or representation of a word, one can change the impact it might have in a matter. I remember watching a movie about the history of Texas. There was one woman who proved to be instrumental in some of the major events surrounding the state's fight for independence from Mexico. When the history book came out, the woman's part was conspicuously missing. Upon commenting on the obvious absence of her name and deeds, it was pointed out that men wrote the history. Remember, it was men who translated the Word of God. How much these men might have let personal bias affect them is a matter of speculation, but the results can be somewhat clearly seen in the confusion, misunderstandings, and divisions that a few Scriptures have created in this area.

We are about to consider the few Scriptures that have been used to put women in their so-called "place" in the kingdom of God. As we consider these Scriptures in light of the whole Word of God, we must consider if any liberty was possibly taken in regard to these Scriptures.

As you are about to see, these Scriptures will be considered from various points. As these different points are brought out, we each must conclude that these

---

[8] Women in Today's Church, page 16

Scriptures must not be taken at face value. Rather, they must be discerned in light of Spirit and truth.

Obviously, these few Scriptures could put women in bondage, but the rest of the Written Word does not condone such bondage. These Scriptures could justify prejudice towards women, but the whole counsel of the Word of God never makes such sins of the heart or attitudes justifiable. Such Scriptures could encourage ignorance towards the ways of God, but the knowledge of the character and attitude of Jesus would reveal such ignorance as darkness.

We must allow the truth of God's character and ways test these few Scriptures. It is from this basis that we can be assured of properly being impacted by His character and attitude towards a matter, and not by our own conclusions. Remember that we will not only be judged for what we believe, but for what is truly in our hearts.

We can also put religious cloaks over the prejudice and hardness of our hearts, but they will not hide our real attitude about a matter. This was brought out in an encounter I had with a man over this very subject.

I had thought this man to be godly. He appeared to stand for truth. Although I had a couple of "red flags" go up when I met him, I just accredited his indifferent attitude to his frustration. He seemed hard, skeptical, and unreceptive towards the moving of the Spirit. Later, I realized my "red flags" were clearly warning me that this man had some unresolved issues in his life.

These unresolved issues made him hard about matters that challenged his personal perception. Ultimately, in his mind, he became the final authority on Scriptural issues, proving that he was unteachable and cruel when challenged to reconsider his attitude and presentation.

This man's real attitude was brought out over the issue of women in ministry. If a woman's writing and teachings were referenced by heretics, he basically blamed these men's heretical views on the woman's influence. In other words, if a woman was spiritually involved in any man's spiritual development, she was to blame for any of his spiritual deviation from the truth. It was as if man cannot be really held responsible for his moral or scriptural deviation as long as a woman could be found to blame.

If you questioned this man about my perception of him, he might deny my conclusion, but his attitude and handling of our disagreement spoke volumes about his inward disposition and spirit. Later, he even wrote his opinions about this matter. In his writing, he clearly was taking liberty in using Scripture to justify his ungodly attitude. His lovely wife even backed him up in another article. Needless to say, regardless of her sincerity about this matter, would she dare to even disagree with him?

Perhaps this man is loving and respectable to his wife. However, such respect may hinge on her totally agreeing with him. Obviously, the man's reaction reveals that he has unresolved issues of the heart. Whether his attitude towards women is a matter of prejudice, cultural conditioning, traumatic experiences, or wrong teaching, the man has taken liberty with Scripture to justify his miserable attitude in his own eyes.

For us, it was not just a matter of agreeing to disagree; it was a matter of having no basis of agreement at the point of spirit. We know a person by their fruit. Obviously, if the right spirit is in place, the fruit and agreement will be there, in spite of the disagreement. Ultimately, the attitude of Jesus and not man's opinions will be exalted, bringing agreement and peace.

The question is, are we willing to truthfully consider these few Scriptures from different angles in light of the complete counsel of God's Word? The purpose for such examination is to reveal wrong thinking, attitudes, and conduct. Will truth be opposed by hiding behind wrong spirits and wickedness? It is our choice whether we choose to love truth or give way to our own selfish preferences and conclusions.

5

THE TRUTH ABOUT MARRIAGE

Since we have discussed attitudes and whether woman was cursed or blessed in the garden, we can begin to consider the implications of women in marriage. Sadly, the attitude towards women, even in marriage, can be traced back to Eve. As Christians we must ensure that we have the mind of Christ concerning this subject.

Through many years of attending different churches, I have often found the emphasis concerning marriage centers around the woman's responsibility to submit. The motivation of this focus can often be traced back to Genesis 3:16.

This lopsided presentation has given the husband an unfair and, at times, abusive leverage. To know whether teachings and attitudes about marriage need to be re-examined, simply observe the condition of marriages within the Church.

Sadly, statistics reveal the world is reflected within the Church where divorce and remarriage are concerned. Domestic violence and abuse are not unheard of among churchgoers. The marriage bed has become defiled by sexual practices encouraged by perversion such as pornography.[1] This perversion has invaded the minds of those who refuse to separate themselves from the world's entanglements. The result is the destruction of this sacred institution.

God established the first principle governing marriage before the fall of man in the garden. Jesus reiterated this principle in Matthew 19:4-5, "…Have ye not read that he who made them at the beginning, made them male and female; And said, For this cause shall a man leave father and mother, and shall cleave to his wife, and they twain shall be one flesh?"

Let us examine what this verse actually says. First of all, it is the man who is to initially leave his family and be united to his wife. It amazes me that many can quote this scripture in reference to marriage and still believe it is the woman who must initially give up all to please her husband. Granted, Psalm 45:10, tells the woman to forget her people. Obviously, to be made one with her husband, the woman must cleave to him as well. But clearly it is up to parents to ensure that the husband will regard their daughter in a proper way before they release her to his care.

Archaeologists have actually found evidence that reveals early civilizations practiced the principle of marriage God laid down in the garden. The matriarchs, as well as the patriarchs, influenced these early people. It was

---

[1] Hebrews 13:4

the woman who held the household property; therefore, kinship came through her.[2]

Professor Flinders Petrie, an archaeologist, made this statement, "The early ideal in the East was separate worlds of men and women while women retained their own rights and property."

These findings would indeed throw doubt on accepted attitudes and beliefs governing women in marriage today. All too often, it has been assumed that women must give up everything for the man's pleasures. But we must keep in mind that it was Eve who moved herself out from under the protection of her Creator to come under the rule of her husband. The result of her action has allowed Satan to use husbands who lack love as a tool to demean the dignity and importance of women, not only in marriage, but also in the kingdom of God.

We can see why God set down this principle. It keeps the woman under the protection of her parents, protected from abusive and harsh husbands. This rule governed the customs of great people of the Bible such as Jacob and Samson. In Genesis 31, for example, we see Jacob going to his wives and explaining his need to separate himself from their father. In Genesis 31:14-16, we find the women making the final decision about taking their children and following him,

> And Rachel and Leah answered and said unto him, Is there yet any <u>portion</u> or <u>inheritance</u> <u>for</u> <u>us</u> <u>in</u> <u>our</u> <u>father's</u> <u>house</u>? Are we not counted of him as

---

[2] God's Word to Women; study notes 53, 58-62

strangers? For he hath sold us, and hath quite devoured also <u>our</u> money. For all the riches which God hath taken from our father, <u>that is ours</u>, and <u>our</u> children's; now then, whatsoever God hath said unto thee, do. (Emphasis added.)

In Samson's situation, we discover that he left his wife in her father's care in Judges 14:19-15:1. We observe in the account of Rebekah that her family had to give permission for her to be taken to Isaac. In Genesis 24:58, we see her family giving her a choice of whether or not she wanted to go.

In the case of the Shunammite woman in 2 Kings 4:8-36 and 8:1-6, we are able to make some interesting observations. In 2 Kings 8:1, we read how the prophet Elisha went to the woman (and not her husband) with the following instruction,

Then spoke Elisha unto the woman, whose son he had restored to life, saying, Arise, and go thou and thine household, and sojourn wheresoever thou canst sojourn; for the LORD hath called for a famine, and it shall also come upon the land seven years.

Nowhere in Scripture is it stated this woman was a widow at this time. In fact, the verse states <u>family</u>, which implies the contrary. 2 Kings 8:2 tells us the woman obeyed and ended up in the land of the Philistines for seven years.

Although the command came from a prophet, a woman executed it. Upon her arrival back in her country, we find her going to the king to request the return of <u>her house and land</u> in 2 Kings 8:5. Due to her identification to the prophet, Elisha, in 2 Kings 8:6, we read the king's response to her, "And when the king asked the woman, she told him. So the king appointed unto her a certain officer, saying, Restore all that was hers, and all the fruits of the field since the day that she left the land, even until now."

This brings us to the subject of marriage in the New Testament. To gain a correct perspective of marriage, one must understand what this sacred institution represents. Marriage is to serve as a representation of the relationship of Christ with His Church. The Apostle Paul confirmed this in Ephesians 5:32, "This is a great mystery, but I speak concerning Christ and the church."

Godly husbands and wives are to become one in spirit, identity, and purpose, just as believers must become one with Christ, and as Christ was one with the Father. To become one means agreement. This implies restoration. Man, once again, becomes complete when united with his particular Eve. Not only is he made whole because he is one with woman who was taken from his side, but, since he is born again, he also now has fellowship with his Creator.

Christians must come to terms with the relationship the Church is to have with Christ. We must examine marriage in light of the example Jesus left for us. Our Christian life and this relationship must function within two godly boundaries—submission and love.

In Ephesians 5:22, a wife is instructed to submit to her husband. According to Roy B. Blizzard, Jr.'s article, submission in this text should be translated as "adapt." "Adapt" has different meanings, but one meaning is to reconcile or bring into one unit.[3] What is the real intent behind godly submission? Submission implies giving way to something that is worthy for the benefit of the whole. No matter how you look at it, submission does not mean coming into subordination under man. After all, there is a difference between submission and subordination.

Pastor W.L. Myers, in his excellent little book entitled *Does God Call Women to Preach?* made this statement, "God did not give man a slave but a help-mate." Women, therefore, must not allow themselves to become subordinate to their husbands.

Women are to submit or adapt to their husbands, <u>as unto the Lord</u>. They must take the example of true submission from Jesus Christ.

Jesus was a submissive servant who served as a perpetual sacrifice before God. He had one goal—to be obedient to the Father. Philippians 2:7-8 confirms this,

> But made himself of no reputation, and took upon him the form of a servant, and was made in the likeness of men; And, being found in fashion as a man, he humbled himself and became obedient unto death, even the death of the cross.

Jesus clearly adapted Himself to carry out the will of the Father. To bring forth a ministry of reconciliation, He had

---

[3] Webster's New Collegiate Dictionary

to take on the disposition of a servant and allow Himself to be fashioned as a man.[4] In light of Jesus' example, wives are being called to a place of servitude, and, like their Lord, they must do all things for the glory of God in that union. They are to live a life of obedience and commitment, not to their husbands, but to their Creator. In a sense, they must become perpetual living sacrifices for the benefit of their families.

A woman must first please God. Godly submission to her husband will be a natural extension of her service to her Lord and Savior. However, if a husband's request proves to be contrary to her Lord, she must submit to the righteousness of her Lord and not the wicked demands of her husband.

Scriptural examples concur with this truth. For example, Abigail's disobedience to her husband prevented King David from committing sin and resulted in saving her entire household. On the other hand, because of her compliance with her husband deceitful ways, Sapphira lost her life.[5]

The Apostle Paul reminded each believer that they must be led by the Spirit of God.[6] This applies to women. The Spirit must instruct us as godly women, as to our ways to ensure an upright attitude, as well as guide us in our examples. As a result, the Apostle Paul made this statement regarding all Christians in Ephesians 5:21, "Submitting yourselves one to another in the fear of God."

---

[4] 2 Corinthians 5:18-19
[5] 1 Samuel 25; Acts 5:1-11
[6] Romans 8:14

Christian living and responses are applicable to all Christians. Submission to his wife must be implemented in the husband's response, just as a wife must love her husband.[7] Love should be the motivation for all responses, and submission is not only a form of honoring someone, but serves as the outward response of godly love. Therefore, love and submission walk hand in hand.

The responsibility of the husband is awesome. He must have the same commitment of love towards his wife as Christ does towards the Church. Christ was first in showing His commitment and devotion to the Church. He gave up His identity to become identified with His Church. Paul brought His commitment to the forefront with this instruction to the husbands in Ephesians 5:25, "Husbands, love your wives, even as Christ also loved the church, and gave himself for it."

A wife's position of servitude stipulates a life that serves as a perpetual living sacrifice on behalf of her family for the glory of God. As for the husband's responsibility, we see an example that goes a step farther. The husband must become the actual sacrifice for the benefit of the family. To be a sacrifice means one gives up their rights and life. Sadly, the focus is usually on the husband's position as the "head" of the family, rather than the sacrificial life he is called to live before his family.

According to *Vine's Expository Dictionary of Biblical Words*, "headship" is not just a position of authority. The other meaning that upholds the intent of this position is

---

[7] Titus 2:4

leadership that is defined and maintained by example. 1 John 4:19 concurs with leadership by example, "We love him, because he first loved us."

Christ's example to His followers persuaded them to follow Him. He was/is not a harsh, demanding dictator. Although He deserves our undivided attention and adoration, He desires us to follow Him because we love Him.

He has left this same example for the husband to follow. A husband's headship is not defined by position, but by the example of love. Adam failed to lead Eve away from temptation and deception. He, in a sense, sacrificed her when it came time to own up to his own actions.

By examining the husband's scriptural responsibility, husbands have been given a second chance to do right by their wives. They must become a sacrifice in order to lead their wives by example in the ways of righteousness.

The Apostle Paul gave this instruction in Ephesians 5:28, "So ought men to love their wives as their own bodies. He that loveth his wife loveth himself."

Men, it is easy to advocate your position in the family, but there is a price. The price is your pride, ego, and worldly leadership. The truest form of spiritual leadership is servitude.[8] Servitude or submission is a product of the love of God working in our hearts. Submission implies sensitivity to the needs of others. Real submission will fulfill Paul's instruction found in Ephesians 5:21.

---

[8] Matthew 20:25-28

Marriage is also representative of both Christ's first and second comings. Bushnell pointed out this truth as follows,

> And then they (Adam and Eve) were separated during a "deep sleep," which came upon Adam. So Christ was with us, and then separated from us by the "deep sleep" of death, while we came, as it were, from His riven side, by faith in His shed blood. Adam was separated, that he might be reunited to Eve, in greater joy than ever, --And one day Christ will come again "to our joy,"—for it was "expedient" for Him to go, and return again, He told us.[9]

The Jewish marriage ceremony also points to the second coming of Christ. The procedure begins with a Shadchan or marriage broker who is hired by parents to find a mate for their son or daughter. Ruth Specter Lascelle relates this procedure to the Father sending the Holy Spirit to draw the spiritual bride to His Son, Jesus Christ.[10]

Bible teacher and author, Zola Levitt, added more insight about the wedding preparation. In his presentation, he shared how the groom had to prepare the honeymoon cottage before the wedding feast could actually take place. Jesus assured his disciples of a similar preparation for the Church in John 14:2-3.

This building project took the better part of a year. Upon completion of the building, the groom's father would make the final determination as to when it was finished. We see

---

[9] God's Word to Women; study notes 50-51
[10] John 16:13-15

this similarity in Christ coming for His Church in Matthew 24:36, "But of that day and hour knoweth no man, no, not the angels of heaven, but my Father only." All the Church can do is wait and be ready for the unexpected arrival of her bridegroom. Jesus confirmed this in Matthew 25:10-13. Only those with the oil of the Holy Spirit will be prepared for the coming of the bridegroom.

Do our attitudes and responses uphold the sanctity of marriage? Are they motivated by the love of God or by prejudice and hatred that hide behind self-righteousness and a few misconstrued scriptures? Christians must examine their position concerning marriage. After all, it is symbolic of the type of relationship the Creator desires with man now, and will consummate in the future.

6

UNVEILING THE TRUTH

The Apostle Paul made this statement in 2 Corinthians 13:8, "For we can do nothing against the truth, but for the truth."

Jesus is the summary of all truth.[1] In the end, truth will either justify or judge man. Therefore, each of us must ask ourselves whether rejection of truth at any level of our Christian life ultimately means we will miss our Savior. Rev. Payne-Smith made this statement, "Give men what proof you will, but seldom do they find more than what it suits them to find. If what is said agrees with their preconceived notions, well; if not, they reject it."

I have had no illusions while writing this book about those who have already made normal, convenient and selfish determinations concerning the subject of women in the Church. I realize the saying, "A man persuaded against his will, is of the same opinion still," remains true today. My goal is to simply educate those who are struggling with this issue and who desire God's perspective. Admittedly, women are not the only ones desiring illumination on this matter, any more than men are the only culprits in stifling

---

[1] John 14:6

women from being what God wants them to be in His kingdom.

Three most quoted scriptures that put women in their so-called "proper place" in the Church promote bondage, while denying human dignity. These verses have been used to hammer women into a box which some refuse to be reconciled to.

The result is these women are accused of being rebellious or of having a "Jezebel Spirit" if they fail to come into compliance with the box that has been established for them. In the next three chapters, we will be examining these scriptures, but first we must examine the attitude of the one who wrote the instructions.

The writer of the verses in question was the Apostle Paul. In Galatians 3:26-29, we have already made reference to the Apostle Paul's attitude towards the issue of women in the kingdom of God,

> For ye are <u>all</u> the children of God by <u>faith in Christ Jesus</u>. For as many of you as have been baptized into Christ have put on Christ. There is neither Jew nor Greek, there is neither bond nor free, there is neither <u>male</u> nor <u>female</u>; for <u>ye are all one</u> in Christ Jesus.

If we belong to Christ, we are heirs of God's promise, thereby establishing equality among all believers. In Galatians 5:1, we see that the culmination of Paul's desire for all believers is that they maintain their freedom in Christ. The harsh reality is that there are so many people who want to bring us into bondage one way or the other. The main reason that individuals want to bring others into oppression is because they are in some way oppressed.

Obviously, the Apostle Paul was fighting for the liberty of all believers. He made no distinction in the case of women. In fact, we see him commending women for laboring in the Gospel.[2] In 1 Corinthians 9:5, we see him defending himself for having a woman as part of his traveling ministry team. But, in 1 Corinthians 11:1-16, 14:34-35, and 1 Timothy 2:9-15, we see instructions which appear contrary to the liberty Paul had so adamantly stood for in his letter to the Galatians. Did Paul have a change of heart, or are there explanations that will not only maintain his attitude, but will ensure continuity with the rest of the Word of God?

There are explanations. They involve understanding cultural and historical events surrounding the people these letters were addressed to. Now, keep in mind that Paul was addressing real people and real problems. For instance, if he were to write a letter to the church in America today, what issues would he address, and would they be applicable to people who might live a hundred years from now? If such a letter was written and Christ tarried, would it bring understanding or confusion to future generations if they did not first consider the problems and times to which it was addressed to ensure the intent and principle of a spiritual matter?

This is why confusion exists over the instructions in question. In order for people to have the correct

---

[2] Romans 16:1-3, 12-13

perspective, they must first understand the issues and problems confronting these different bodies of believers.

In the case of the Corinthian Church, their greatest influence and distraction came from those trying to bring in Judaism. If the Judaizers were successful, it would mean bondage for the believers.

The Apostle Paul was, therefore, contending with Jewish traditions, something he was quite familiar with because of having been a Pharisee. In fact, we see him clearly referring to two distinct laws in his first letter to the Corinthians. In 1 Corinthians 9:9 he referred to the Law of Moses (the Torah), while in 1 Corinthians 14:34 he was clearly referring to another law.

The other law he referred to in this text has already been highlighted in this book. It is known as the Oral Law of the Jews. The Oral Law was a re-interpretation, explanation, and addition of the Mosaic Law. These re-interpretations became traditions that were adhered to, even though they were simply re-interpretations or explanations of a Law that clearly stood on its own merits. This particular law was directed at issues that affected the Jewish people's daily life. As previously stated, the Oral Law of the Jews was passed down orally until it was written down in 100 A.D. The writing became known as the Mishnah, the Palestinian, or the Babylonian Talmud.[3]

Jesus referred to the effect that Jewish tradition had on those who followed them in Matthew 23:4, 5a and 13,

---

[3] Difficult Sayings (article)

For they bind heavy burdens and grievous to be borne, and lay them on men's shoulders, but they themselves will not move them with one of their fingers. But all their works they do to be seen of men...But woe unto you, scribes and Pharisees, hypocrites! For ye shut up the kingdom of heaven against men; for ye neither go in yourselves, neither suffer them that are entering to go in.

If improperly interpreted or applied, these Jewish traditions had the means to show extreme prejudice against women and treat them as cursed. Ruth Specter Lascelle confirmed this prejudice when sharing about her orthodox Jewish upbringing. Her grandfather would say a prayer that all orthodox Jewish men repeat. It goes like this:

> Blessed art Thou, O Lord our God, King of the Universe Who hath not created me a <u>slave</u>.
> Blessed are Thou, O Lord our God, King of the Universe Who hath not created me a <u>Gentile</u>.
> Blessed are Thou, O Lord our God, King of the Universe Who hath not created me a <u>woman</u>.[4]

This attitude was never upheld or condoned by the Written Law. In fact, we see Jesus condemning Jewish traditions, but He both quoted and fulfilled the Written Law. We must not forget about the Apostle Paul. He was a Pharisee, and, in Galatians 3:28, he reversed this whole

---

[4] Also see Jewish Faith and the New Covenant, page 53

concept. He stated that, in Christ, there is neither _bond_ nor free, Jew nor _Gentile_, male nor _female_. [5]

In 1 Corinthians 11:1-16, Paul was dealing with the Jewish custom of veiling. The men wore what they called a tallith or prayer shawl. This shawl was both a sign of reverence before God and of condemnation of sin. In 1 Corinthians 11:4, Paul condemned this practice. He stated, "Every man praying or prophesying, having his head covered, dishonoreth his head." Who is the head of man? The Apostle Paul answered that question in the previous Scripture, Jesus Christ.

You must compare Scripture with Scripture to understand the real implication behind Paul's instruction. We know there is no condemnation for those who are in Christ Jesus and are walking after the Spirit; therefore, there is no shame.[6]

In his internet article, Blizzard tells us that "head" in 1 Corinthians 11:3 means image or reflection. We know that Moses covered the heavenly reflection displayed by his countenance when he came down from the mountain, but we are told in 2 Corinthians 3:18 that we are to reflect the Lord's glory.[7]

In the case of women, it was a different issue. Women did not practice veiling. The Old Testament only records two events where women veiled themselves. Rebekah put on a veil when she first saw Isaac, possibly to show reverence for the sorrow he felt over his mother's death.

---

[5] Matthew 5:17-20; 22:34-40
[6] Romans 8:1; 1 Corinthians 2:11-14
[7] Consider 2 Corinthians 3:13-18

Tamar used a veil to keep Judah from recognizing her. It is interesting to note that Judah mistook Tamar for a prostitute because her face was veiled. Remember, being veiled implied sin and guilt, and Christ took away sin and guilt on the cross.[8]

It tells us man is head of the woman. But we must note the term "man" is used, and not husband. Who is the head of the woman in marriage and in ministry? It is the Man, not a man. In other words, it is the man, Christ Jesus. Granted, godly women have a responsibility to give way to their husbands in a godly way, but they will still reflect the glory of their Lord.

According to 1 Corinthians 11:6, Paul gave the woman liberty to choose whether she wanted to wear a veil or not. He implied that if she wore a veil, she must understand it represented neither reverence nor guilt. Once again, we are reminded that the veil was taken away so all of Jesus' followers could reflect Him. It is the life of Christ in every believer that serves as the light to those who are lost.

Here we have the truth behind veiling. All Christians must reflect Christ, and not their personal best. If they hide behind a veil, the light of Christ cannot shine forth to serve as a living testimony.[9] With this in mind, what about the credibility of the other instructions concerning women in 1 Corinthians 11:1-16? We once again see reference to "headship" in the New Testament. One of its meanings is leadership through example. However, according to

---

[8] Genesis 24:65; 38:14-15; 2 Corinthians 5:21
[9] Matthew 5:14

Bushnell, "head" in the Old Testament means first in order.[10]

The usage of "head" in 1 Corinthians 11:3 illuminates its simplicity in Scripture, for man was created first, then woman. Ethel Ruff, an ordained Baptist minister, made this interesting observation about the order of creation in her book, *When the Saints Go Marching,*

> So it was that the human pair, 'them,' originally had dominion. That man was placed here first is no proof of his superiority, <u>for creation was in the ascending order, lowest to the highest, and Eve came last</u>. It has been argued that man was superior in intellect, for he named the beasts, birds, etc. But Eve named her children. *(Genesis 4:25, emphasis added.)*

Let us just say for a moment that the term "head" points to superiority and subordination. Here is another interesting observation about the concept of "head" in 1 Corinthians 11:3. We are told God is the head of Christ, yet Philippians 2:9 tells us, "Wherefore, God also hath highly exalted him, and given him a name which is above every name."

Jesus in His humanity reflected the glory of the Father. He not only was equal with the Father, He existed before all creation, and was willing to come into a place of submission to His Father.

God exalted Christ. Christ, the head of man, became a servant to man. We see this in His example in John 13:3-

---

[10] God's Word to Women, study note 276

15. How can man, therefore, exalt himself above his wife and claim to be her superior, especially when he is commanded, in 1 Peter 3:7, to give her honor as unto a weaker vessel to ensure that his prayers will not be hindered. To properly give his wife honor, he would have to humble himself and prefer her betterment over his personal desires and needs.

We can debate "headship" where woman is concerned, but there is only one true "head" over all believers in relationship to authority, Jesus Christ.[11] It was Christ who purchased the Church with His blood. Therefore, every Christian owes Him complete adoration and commitment. Every Christian should bring glory to Him.

But some may argue, a woman must be in subjection to her husband. According to Bushnell, subjection does not mean obedience, but rather a yielding up of one's will or rights in preference to another.[12] This definition is consistent with the instructions found in Romans 12:10-11 in relationship to honoring one another in brotherly love, and in Ephesians 5:21 where each believer must submit to one another out of the fear of the Lord.

Another subject of debate has been the length of a woman's hair. 1 Corinthians 11:15 states, "But if a woman have long hair, it is a glory to her; for her hair is given her for a covering." Paul was asking a question and not making a statement.

---

[11] Ephesians 4:15
[12] God's Word to Women, study note 293

Hair cannot possibly serve as a woman's spiritual covering or determine her level of commitment to God or her husband. Granted, it can be a source that reflects or enhances her beauty, but it should never hold any place of authority. According to scripture, it is God who covers the head in the day of battle, and the Holy Spirit is the One who serves as the real covering over God's saints. If anything is to cover the Christian's head, it must be the spiritual helmet of salvation.[13]

Clearly, the Apostle Paul was contending with Jewish customs in 1 Corinthians 11. We actually see him referring to these as customs in 1 Corinthians 11:16. He made this comment, "But if any man seem to be contentious, we have no such custom, neither the churches of God." Can you clearly grasp his message? He stated there is no such custom, especially in the churches. It is easy to see Paul was refuting Jewish customs that did not represent the real spirit, heart, or mind of the new Church.

The Law given to Moses was to lead people to Christ. Many of the Jewish customs and practices served as shadows that pointed to Jesus Christ. To argue over these issues and to insist that people adhere to them would not only be unprofitable, but it would be putting grievous burdens that had no ability to neither impact a person's spirit nor change their life.[14]

There is confusion regarding 1 Corinthians 11:1-16. We could debate the meanings behind each scripture, but the

---

[13] Psalm 140:7; Isaiah 30:1; Ephesians 6:17; 1 Thessalonians 5:8
[14] Acts 15:19-20; Galatians 3:21-24; 4:9-10; Colossians 2:16-17; Titus 3:9

conclusion would be the same: it was a matter of Jewish customs and not the inspiration of the Holy Spirit. These passages are in stark contrast to the rest of Scripture. As Christians, we have no agreement with beliefs that take away from the message of Christ and put people in bondage. It is time we focused on the truth governing all Christians.

Ruth Specter Lascelle found liberty from Jewish traditions when she met her Messiah. She spent many years serving her Savior and Lord as a missionary, evangelist, Bible teacher, and author. In response to the Jewish Orthodox prayer she heard from her grandfather throughout her early years, she penned this testimony,

> After I became a believer in the Lord Jesus as my Messiah, I could recreate that prayer that my grandfather prayed and which Paul prayed (before his conversion) and which orthodox Jewish men today pray—
>
> Blessed art Thou, O Lord our God, King of the Universe Who hath recreated me and I am no longer a slave (to sin).
>
> Blessed art Thou, O Lord our God, King of the Universe Who hath recreated me and I am no longer a heathen.
>
> Blessed art Thou, O Lord our God, King of the Universe Who hath recreated me and I am now a SON OF GOD!

Men and women have the same inheritance in the kingdom of God. The truth that must govern us, as believers, is the reality that men and women are all "sons or children," bought with the precious blood of Jesus. How can Christians quibble about superiority and importance when being a "child of God" should be considered the greatest position an individual holds? This position not only determines our relationship here on earth with our Creator, but also guarantees us a heavenly inheritance for eternity.

7

RESTRAINT OR PERSECUTION?

In 1 Timothy 2:9-15, we see Paul's instructions concerning women's dress and conduct. We could accept these scriptures at face value and settle for their implication without question. However, would our interpretation of these verses be consistent with the entire Word of God?

A few questions need to be asked before we examine these verses. Paul never advocated a dress code anywhere else in scripture, so why here? Both knowledge and attitude will not only always inspire conduct for women, but men as well. This is evident throughout Scripture. But, why make such an emphasis of it with this body of believers? Is there an explanation that will put this focus in perspective?

The answer is yes. There were cultural issues and possibly circumstances that called for wise restraint on the part of the women who belonged to this particular body. With this in mind, let us examine these scriptures in light of the rest of the Word of God and the times in which these people lived. 1 Timothy 2:9 states, "In like manner, also, that women adorn themselves in modest, apparel, with shamefacedness and sobriety, not with broided hair, or gold, or pearls, or costly array."

When we consider other Scriptures, we know that God does not look at the outward appearance of man. The Apostle Peter talked about the need for women to possess inward beauty, rather than outward vanity. Solomon declared that charm is deceptive and beauty fleeing, but a woman who fears God should be praised.[1]

Since dress is no more an indication of Christianity than are religious acts, we must take time to consider if there were events that deemed these instructions necessary. According to my studies there are a couple of possibilities.

This letter was written to Timothy who was overseeing the Church at Ephesus. Ephesus was famed for its heresies and female supremacy in various cults. For example, there were temple prostitutes at the shrine of Diana that wore outlandish apparel. Naturally, the apostle would want Christian women to remain distinct from such associations.[2]

Another explanation has to do with historical events. There were dangerous circumstances that were developing that required extremely wise decisions on the part of the Church. These wise responses could mean life or death for the believers.

Nero was in power in Rome at the time the Apostle Paul wrote this letter. Nero's second wife was a Jewess and

---

[1] 1 Samuel 16:7; Proverbs 31:30; 1 Peter 3:3-4
[2] Difficult Sayings (article)

supported the Oral Law of the Jews. Because of her belief, she hated Christians. Needless to say, her hatred influenced policy and attitudes that resulted in the severe persecution of Christians. This hatred and persecution were clearly reinforced when Nero blamed Christians for his own actions resulting in the burning of Rome. After this false accusation, the persecution of Christians escalated into unspeakable atrocities.

This persecution penetrated the outer areas of the Roman Empire. One of the cities within reach of Rome was Ephesus. We must understand that women did find liberty in Christ. This liberty brought a change in dress and conduct that was decisively different from their Jewish counterparts.

According to Pastor George Watkins, Roman soldiers watched for women who displayed a change in dress and conduct. If they spotted a woman with such freedom, they would follow her in hopes of discovering the church. This could spell persecution and death for members of God's family.[3]

It was also pointed out that "professing" in 1 Timothy 2:10 is "epaggellomai" and was also in regard to those who were offering promises through public speaking, such as political candidates and false teachers.[4] If Christian women were publicly speaking in regards to salvation, Paul could be instructing them to be discrete and distinct,

---

[3] Women in Today's Church, pages 26-27
[4] Difficult Sayings (article), Consider Strong's Concordance, #1861 and 2 Peter 2:19

confirming their testimony by godly works, and not outward vanity.

Clearly, Paul was telling Christian women to dress in a moderate way to maintain an inner distinction as to their witness, as well as for their possible protection. Obviously, Paul's instructions show godly wisdom that all Christian women should adhere to. God is interested in inward beauty and not outward vanity. As a result, there must be a distinction from the world's idea of beauty and the right attitude that will outshine all vanity and become an attraction to those who are lost.

This brings us to the next instruction found in 1 Timothy 2:11, "Let the woman learn in silence with all subjection." Under Jewish tradition, women were not allowed to learn about Scriptural matters. As new converts in Christ, these women were given the necessary liberty to learn about their God. What does it mean to learn in silence?

"Silence" in this Scripture could be better translated as "a calm quietness."[5] To effectively learn, there must be quietness of the mind to listen, hear, and retain. There are so many activities that can rob, kill, and destroy the impact of the Word. It was also pointed out that learning requires asking questions, but all conduct must be done in an orderly manner.[6] Once again, Christian women are called to show discretion and restraint in their conduct.

According to other scriptures, these women were not to remain passive students. Teaching in God's kingdom has

---

[5] Ibid, consider #2271
[6] 1 Corinthians 14:33

two goals that produce action and results. These goals are found in Ephesians 4:11-13. They are to prepare God's people for service and to bring them to spiritual maturity. These goals can be summarized in the concept of edification.

Christians, regardless of gender, must be brought to maturity in order to discern good and evil. The writer of Hebrews actually rebuked believers who refused to come to such maturity.[7]

There must never be a professional student in the kingdom of heaven. Instruction should bring a Christian to a life of service, which brings glory to their Lord and edifies the Body. By obeying these instructions, believers will begin to exemplify Christ and His righteousness in their lives. According to Romans 8:29, Christians have been predestined to be conformed to the very image of Christ.

1 Timothy 2:12-14 states,
> But I suffer not a woman to teach, nor to usurp authority over the man, but to be in silence. For Adam was first formed, then Eve. And Adam was not deceived, but the woman being deceived, was in the transgression.

There has been much controversy and abuse surrounding these verses. The first abuse can be found with the first sentence of 1 Timothy 2:12, which states that a woman must not teach. It is important to point out that in 2:11 the word "the" woman was used and here the word

---

[7] Hebrews 5:11-14

"a" woman was used. Both words imply there was a single female involved in the controversy.

Some believe, such as Skip Moen, these references point to "a particular woman" who was usurping authority in the church. Even though Paul does not mention a particular name, those at Ephesus would have known who he was talking about.

Consider the church of Thyatira in Revelation 2:18-23. There was a woman in the church who was referred to as a "Jezebel." She was identified as being a false prophetess who had much influence in the church. In this case a single woman is being called out, but there is not further rebuke or instruction that all women need to be silenced. It is clear that women played a part in teaching, exhorting, and imparting the word.

Many have gone into extremes when interpreting the Scriptures in 1 Timothy to mean women are not to teach even in Sunday school. This is unrealistic and unscriptural. We are reminded of Titus 2:3-4, that the older women are to teach the younger women proper conduct towards their husbands and children. This clearly involves taking authority over others.

The Apostle Paul commended Timothy's grandmother and mother in 2 Timothy 1:5 for their influence on Timothy's life. Acts 18:26 tells us that Priscilla, along with her husband, taught Apollos the way of God in a more adequate manner. In these scriptures, we see women instructing and influencing women, children, and men.

These scriptural truths hint at another meaning behind this instruction. What is it? Let us continue to examine these verses. The next instruction is: "...nor to usurp authority over the man..." In the King James Version, the word "usurp" is added to this scripture.

Pastor W. L. Myers stated in his book that this instruction can only be applied to husbands and wives. He reproved those who refused to see the singular tense of both genders in this verse. He declared the real meaning of this instruction is, "No woman (wife) can usurp authority over the man, her husband." This is consistent to Paul's instruction about husbands and wives in Ephesians 5.

Myers also insisted that the word "usurp" does not mean what many perceive it to mean. He declared the word "usurp" means to take possession by force. The woman must not lord a matter over her husband or demand total subjection.

This could be correct, but does it run consistent with the rest of the text in this chapter? In his article, "Difficult Sayings," Jonathan Went, discussed the word "authority" in this Scripture.

The Greek word for it is "authentein," which means, "one acting by his own authority, or being dominating." Although "authentein" is never used in the other places where Paul speaks of authority, this Scripture is basically denouncing a woman from acting out of control or intentionally without being in proper submission to her husband or father.

However, we must remember that, according to the complete text, the Apostle Paul was not making reference to husbands and wives in these Scriptures, but Church conduct. In her explanation of this series of verses, Bushnell stated the purpose of these scriptures was simply for the protection of women.[8]

The Jews were angered at the prospect of women being educated. The apostle was stating that, if a woman was sincere about learning, she had a right to do so, but she must do it in meekness to ensure order and not draw attention to herself. At the same time, he also put a restraint on women teaching men due to the perilous times in which they lived as a means to protect them from the long reach of Rome, as well as the local church.

In her response to the word "usurp," Bushnell stated it cannot be found in the original text, therefore one must conclude it has been added.[9]

Although Moen, Bushnell, Myers, and Went had different approaches to explain the meaning of these scriptures, they had the same conclusion. The popular interpretation of these scriptures by the Church today is contrary to the spirit and truth of the Word, and must be challenged.

1 Timothy 2:14 states, "And Adam was not deceived, but the woman, being deceived was in the transgression." My conclusion is that this scripture focuses on the real purpose behind this series of instructions in 1 Timothy. The

---

[8] God's Word to Women, study notes 336-337
[9] Ibid, study note 337

issue inspiring these verses was the woman's right and need to learn. 1 Timothy 2:14 reinforces this by reminding us that Eve was deceived.

We must take this one step further by asking ourselves, "Why was Eve deceived?" Hosea 4:6 tells us that people perish from lack of knowledge. Ephesians 4:14 instructs people to cease being children and become mature in their knowledge of the Lord so they will no longer be tossed to and fro by every changing wind of doctrine.

Eve was deceived because she lacked the proper instruction. The only way to prevent this from occurring again was to guarantee women the right to receive instruction. Therefore, the rules of conduct put forth in the letter to Timothy were not to put women in total subjection to men, but to secure their right to learn in the midst of cultures that were critical of such learning, while ensuring their safety.

The last scripture attached to these instructions is 1 Timothy 2:15. It states, "Notwithstanding, she shall be saved in childbearing, if they continue in faith and charity and holiness with sobriety." Many have interpreted this scripture to mean that salvation will come to women if they have children. Many cults have practiced this, resulting in abuse. However, Christians should know that the scripture is in reference to the seed of the woman, Jesus Christ.[10]

It amazes me that Paul would once again make reference to woman's part in salvation. It is as though he

---

[10] Genesis 3:15

wanted to reiterate the importance of woman in the plan of salvation.

Christ came to earth via woman (Mary), and it is only through Christ that redemption can be obtained. How could man consider woman to be less important than he? After all, God used a woman, not a man, to bring forth His plan of salvation in the form of His Son. If it was not for the woman, man would still be miserably lost.

To add an interesting note, it is believed by some that 1 Timothy 2:11-12 was added 115 AD, fifty years after Paul's martyrdom.[11] If this is true, clearly liberty has been taken with God's Word. But, even if the liberty was not taken, what would the Apostle Paul say to the Church today concerning their handling of this passage of Scripture? Would he be appalled at the knowledge that words he penned to protect and ensure women the right to learn are now being used by some of the Church to oppress, persecute, and enslave them? What a sad irony this would be to a man who fought long and hard for spiritual liberty for all the children of God.

---

[11] Difficult Sayings (article)

8

BETWEEN A ROCK AND A HARD PLACE

In response to the treatment of women in the church, Pastor George Watkins of Mt. Vernon, Washington began the introduction of his small book *Women in Today's Church* by stating that 50 percent of God's Church is being held in bondage by generations of misunderstanding and misinterpretation. He was referring to women's place and role in the kingdom of God. Watkins maintained that if liberty was afforded to the women of God, it would result in 100 percent destruction of the kingdom of Satan.

I must admit the Bible calls Satan the god of this age and he will rule his unseen kingdom until Jesus puts him under his feet. However, Watkins brings out an important point as to the Church's ability and power as a body and an army to properly stand against the inroads of this enemy when one part of it is being oppressed.

The title of this particular chapter is not only a cliché, but also a description of what women must confront in order to serve God. Often condemned by man if she does, and disobedient to God if she does not, women find themselves struggling to overcome obstacles their male counterparts do not encounter in a life of service. It is as though women have been destined to only be seen and not heard in the Church. The final product has weakened the Church and strengthened Satan's work.

We have already examined two sets of controversial scriptures in regard to women. Now, let us consider the last of these controversial Scriptures. 1 Corinthians 14:34-35 states,

> Let your women keep silence in the churches; for it is not permitted unto them to speak, but they are commanded to be under obedience, as also saith the law. And if they will learn anything, let them ask their husbands at home; for it is a shame for women to speak in the church.

Once again, we are confronted with what could be considered an unshakable rule governing women in the Church. However, we must observe these verses in light of the rest of God's Word.

In 1 Corinthians 14:26, we begin to see the accepted and popular interpretation of these two scriptures losing credibility as part of the inspired text, "How is it, then, brethren? When ye come together, every one of you hath a psalm, hath a doctrine, hath a tongue, hath a revelation, hath an interpretation. Let all things be done unto edifying." (Emphasis added)

We know terms such as the "sons of God" and "brothers or brethren" apply to both men and women. If it is difficult for a person to accept that the instruction of verse 26 also applies to women, but all we need to do is refer them to the words "every one." Note that this scripture verse had to have been written a few minutes before verses 34-35. Did the Apostle Paul suddenly change his mind about women having the liberty to operate in their spiritual gifts?

Some maintain that verses 34 and 35 are only applicable for husbands and wives. This may be a quick way to bring the discussion to an end, but what about single women? Where do they fit in Church protocol?

The Apostle Paul clearly dealt with the subject of single women in 1 Corinthians 7:25 and 34,

> Now concerning virgins, I have no commandment of the Lord; yet I give my judgment, as one that hath obtained mercy of the Lord to be faithful...There is difference also between a wife and a virgin. The unmarried woman careth for the things of the Lord, that she may be holy both in body and in spirit; but she that is married careth for the things of the world, how she may please her husband.

There is no instruction for the single woman to remain silent or come under the control of man. In fact, Paul commended unmarried women for their devotion solely to the Lord. If 1 Corinthians 7:34-35 were only applicable to married women, does it mean God excludes married women from speaking in the church when it comes to their spiritual gifts?

Acts 2:17-18 declares,

> And it shall come to pass in the last days, saith God, I will pour out of my Spirit upon all flesh; and

your sons and your <u>daughters</u> shall prophesy, and your young men shall see visions, and your old men shall dream dreams; And on my servants and on my <u>handmaidens</u> I will pour out in those days of my Spirit, and they shall prophesy. (Emphasis added.)

There is no indication that God was making a distinction based on sex or marital status in this declaration. Both men and women would be moved by the Holy Spirit in prophecy.

Prophecy is when one speaks forth truths to the Church. This was not uncommon in the new Church. This gift was for the edification of the Body and it was not limited to men. Acts 21:9 tells us that Philip had four daughters who had the gift of prophecy. 1 Thessalonians 5:19-20 commands us not to quench the Spirit and despise not prophesyings.

How can a godly woman, married or single, remain silent when prompted by the Holy Spirit? Who would be willing to quench the Spirit? On the other hand, how can all women be strictly accountable to two scriptures that are inconsistent with the rest of the Word?

In Corinthians, we see a pattern. Remember, the apostle Paul was dealing with the infiltration of Judaism into the Corinthian Church. It is believed that Paul referred to another source, such as a letter written to him, which he quotes before writing his stand on these issues. For instance, in 1 Corinthians 8:1 we read, "Now as touching things offered unto idols..."

In 1 Corinthians 10:23, we read a statement that was being quoted and answered, "All things are lawful for me, but all things are not expedient; all things are lawful for me, but all things edify not."

In 1 Corinthians 14:34-35, we can identify this pattern. For instance, let us focus on this statement, "…for it is not permitted unto them to speak…" Paul is not making a command here, but referring to something alien to church conduct. While we may be uncertain of the source Paul was referring to throughout the letter, we are sure of the inspiration behind these two scriptures. Note the last part of verse 14:34, "…as also saith the law."

The Apostle Paul was not stating "our law" or "my law," but "the law." Clearly, the apostle was not laying personal claim to this law in regard to the Church. Therefore, what law was Paul making reference to?

The attitudes toward women in these two verses are clearly in accordance with the Oral Law of the Jews. (Note: remember the Oral Law of the Jews is not contained within the Old Testament.) Paul was quoting the Oral Law of the Jews, the Talmud and not the written Law of Moses, the Torah.

The tradition of the Oral Law was to separate men and women into different sections during religious teaching and worship. Apparently, if an issue confused some women during service, they would disrupt the services by yelling the question to their husbands from their section. To keep order, it was commanded in the Talmud, not the Torah, for women to refrain from asking the question until they were in the confines of their homes. This would be practical protocol when it came to order, but the gifts are a different matter.

It appears as if Paul was referring to the Oral Law of the Jews to give the Corinthians a comparison in regard to order. After all, the theme of 1 Corinthians 14 is about order in the Body when it came to the inspirational gifts of speaking in tongues and prophesies.

Apparently, the Corinthians did not display order in the use of these gifts, and, since they were leaning towards the Oral Law of the Jews, Paul was possibly using it to drive home a point in relationship to order. Clearly, it was not to establish a law for women to keep silent in the middle of establishing the proper order for Church conduct in regards to the use of the gifts of the Holy Ghost.

We ultimately see a blatant rebuke in Paul's next statement which many seem to ignore when using these scriptures to "put women in their place" in God's kingdom. "What? Came the word of God out from you? Or came it unto you only" (1 Corinthians 14:36)? The Apostle Paul was exhorting his hearers to agree with his evaluation about the proper conduct and order as to the instructions he put forth concerning the gifts.

Clearly, Paul's instructions were not about silencing women but making sure those who operated in a gift, man or woman, have liberty to do so but do it in an orderly manner. Scripture is clear, believers must not grieve the Spirit in His work, quench prophecy, or forbid tongues.[1]

---

[1] Ephesians 4:30; 1 Thessalonians 5:19-20; 1 Corinthians 14:39

Who would display such conceit towards godly instruction? In Jesus' condemnation of the teachers of the law and the Pharisees, He referred to them as hypocritical experts of the Law that put people in bondage.[2] Such people missed the whole point because they always missed God's heart in a matter. Paul concluded with this challenge in 1 Corinthians 14:37-38, "If any man think himself to be a prophet, or spiritual, let him acknowledge that the things that I write unto you are the commandments of the Lord. But if any man be ignorant, let him be ignorant."

Needless to say, most people use these couple of Scriptures in 1 Corinthians 14 to determine women's place in the Church, but, if you note, Paul did not end with the subject of women, but with prophesy and tongues. Then, he made this statement, "Let all things be done decently and in order."

The burden of proof in regard to the debate that was evident concerning proper attitudes and practice for the local body at Corinth fell on those who were promoting Jewish traditions. If they were followers of Jesus, they had to prove it by submitting to the instructions Paul set down. If they did not, Paul instructed those around them to leave them in their ignorance.

In the information contained in his article, Went pointed out the similarities between 1 Timothy 2:11-12 and 1 Corinthians 14:35. If the Scriptures in Timothy were added 50 years after Paul's martyrdom, then most likely the same liberty was taken with the couple of inconsistent Scriptures

---

[2] Matthew 1:20; 23

found in 1 Corinthians 14. After all, altering a few Scriptures here or there will not do any real harm, or will it?

However, as we approach 1 Corinthians 14, it must be reiterated that Paul was not establishing a separate law for women. He had already stipulated the one law that all Christians were to adhere to in Romans 8:2, and that is the law of the Spirit of the life in Christ Jesus. We know according to 2 Corinthians 3:17 that wherever the Spirit is there is liberty to move accordingly and not the bondage of man or religion. Whether these Scriptures were added, or Paul was making reference to the Oral Law of the Jews to bring contrast, they were not meant to put women in bondage.

Clearly, the Apostle Paul discredited the attitudes and instructions the Oral Law maintained towards women. Whether his instructions in 1 Corinthians 14 were to make sure everyone, including women, should be allowed to operate in their gifts, or whether he was establishing order as to the usage of gifts or both, he was not laying claim to the practice of keeping women silent as being his law or commandment. Surely, Paul was aware that, even in the Old Testament, women also enjoyed great religious freedom. In one quick swoop of the pen, he put the whole matter into scriptural perspective in Galatians 3:28.

Why is it today that some have a tendency to focus on a few verses, while ignoring the rest? Paul's test remains the same. If someone claims to be spiritual, let them line up with his consistent instructions about church matters. If they do not follow them, then leave them to their preferred ignorance.

Let Romans 12:16 summarize the proper attitude among Christians, regardless of gender, "Be of the same mind one toward another. Mind not high things, but condescend to men of low estate. Be not wise in your own conceits."

9

THE LAST SHALL BE FIRST

What does it mean to be the greatest in the kingdom of heaven? Matthew 20:26b-27 gives us the answer, "...but whosoever will be great among you, let him be your minister, And whosoever will be chief among you, let him be your servant."

Greatness in the kingdom of heaven is not determined by title, position, or rank, but by genuine servitude. As servants of God, Christians become vessels in the hand of the Great Potter, or instruments in the hand of the Great Conductor. After all, it is Christ's life that believers are manifesting, it is the Father's business they must carry out, and it is the power of the Spirit that ensures all spiritual matters are brought to completion. Obviously, it is not a matter of position, rank, or gender, rather it comes down to what we will allow God to do in us, through us, and with us as His vessels and instruments.[1]

---

[1] Luke2:49; 24:49; Romans 6:13-16; 9:20-21; Galatians 2:20

God is clearly not impressed or persuaded by positions. He is no respecter of persons.[2] In fact, God considers Christian attitudes and responses foremost. We see Him guarding against any favoritism in the Church as well. 1 Corinthians 12:22-25 states,

> Nay, much more those members of the body which seem to be more feeble, are necessary: And those members of the body, which we think to be less honorable, upon these we bestow more abundant honor; and our uncomely parts have more abundant comeliness. For our comely parts have no need; but God hath tempered the body together, having given more abundant honor to that part which lacked. That there should be no schism in the body, but that the members should have the same care one for another.

To avoid schisms or divisions in the Body, the Lord exalts those parts that seem less honorable to the same place as the rest of the members of the Body. Obviously, there is no preference, exaltation, or honor given to certain members of the Body, regardless of the preference that may be shown by those who are part of the Church.

We have to keep in mind that God is the potter. He chooses what vessels He will use and how He will use them. Vessels do not hold ranks, nor are they considered on the basis of gender. Such vessels do not make decisions concerning their use, whether in regard to self or to others. Some of the vessels we perceive to be least

---

[2] Romans 2:11; Ephesians 6:9

might be the very vessels God will bestow the greatest honor upon. For other vessels that we would choose to exalt, He may pass by. We judge by the outward appearance, but God's considers the heart.[3]

God is not limited by the vessel He uses. He can use a donkey, as He did in the case of Balaam. He will use young people. For example, it was upon the suggestion of a young Jewish girl that Naaman sought out Elisha for healing. The prophet Jeremiah referred to himself as a child.[4] Luke 2:8-17 tells us the angels pronounced Christ's birth to shepherds who were the first to proclaim that the Messiah was born. Shepherds were considered to be the dregs of society. Imagine what would have happened if any of these individuals had remained silent.

Matthew 3:4 gives us this description of John the Baptist, "And the same John had his raiment of camel's hair, and a leathern girdle about his loins; and his meat was locusts and wild honey." How many of our churches today would accept John the Baptist into their midst, let alone acknowledge him as a prophet?

Jesus initially called fishermen, not merchants or the educated, to follow Him in order to become fishers of men.[5] As for the Apostle Paul, we gain this insight about him in 2 Corinthians 10:10: "For his letters, say they, are weighty and powerful, but his bodily presence is weak, and his speech contemptible."

---

[3] Romans 9:21-23
[4] Numbers 22:28-32; 2 Kings 5:1-15; Jeremiah 1:6
[5] Matthew 4:18-22

In Luke 19:35-40 we read how the Pharisees criticized the people paying homage to Christ. Jesus made this response in Luke 19:40b, "I tell you that, if these should hold their peace, the stones would immediately cry out."

Once again, God will not be limited by the vessels He chooses to use. Some vessels are used for dishonorable purposes like Pharaoh and Judas Iscariot. Other vessels are used for noble purposes like Peter and Paul. The vessels of dishonor are destined for destruction, while the vessels of honor will bring glory to God. The determination of which vessel a person becomes originates with their heart response towards God. Noble vessels have an available heart to God and will allow themselves to be set apart for His use and glory.

2 Timothy 2:19-22 talks about the different vessels in the house of God. Some of these vessels are made of gold and silver, but some of wood and clay. The use of these vessels may be honorable or dishonorable, but those who desire to be used in an honorable way must cleanse themselves and submit to the Holy Spirit. It is the Spirit of God that will make a vessel holy and useful for the Master's use, ready to do any good work.

The Apostle Paul gave us insight in these Scriptures in 2 Timothy as to how to cleanse ourselves, "Flee also youthful lusts, but follow righteousness, faith, charity, peace with them that call on the Lord out of a pure heart" (2 Timothy 2:22).

Our God is sovereign. He decides who He will use and how He will use each vessel. 1 Corinthians 12:11 and 18 confirms this same type of sovereign work within the Church, "But all these worketh that one and the selfsame Spirit, dividing to every man severally as he will…But now hath God set the members, <u>every</u> one of them in the body, as it hath pleased him." (Emphasis added.) The question is what part of our own body can be distinguished as male and what part as female? Like our body, when it comes to the Body of Christ, there is no such distinction.

The real issue in the kingdom of God is not <u>what type of vessel</u> God chooses to use, but whether a vessel is <u>being used</u> by God. The real test of the vessel does not rest with status, rank, or gender, but with the <u>message</u>.

If God wants to use a vessel that might be unacceptable to man, He will do so in spite of man's unwillingness to accept it. After all, it is not up to God to lower His ways to compliment man's prideful, vain perception, but, rather, it is up to man to first humble himself in preparation in order to adjust his base ways to the higher purpose of God.

God uses the most unlikely vessels as a test to the wise and strong. By using the foolish, weak, base, and despised, He illuminates the true works of darkness in the hearts of men. Decisions that are made as hidden works of darkness are exposed. Either the individual will repent of darkness, or they will continue to give way to the darkness of their sin.[6]

This brings us to the subject of God using women in His kingdom. If any one vessel has been classified as being foolish, weak, base, and despised, it has been the woman.

---

[6] John 3:19-21; 1 Corinthians 1:25-29

Although not necessarily earned, this description has been readily placed upon females.

1 Peter 3:7 gives this command, "In like manner, ye husbands, dwell with them according to knowledge, giving honor unto the wife, as unto the weaker vessel, and as being heirs together of the grace of life; that your prayers be not hindered." In this Scripture, we see a reference made concerning woman being the weaker partner. In what way is a woman weaker?

We know that, in the area of physical strength, she is not equal, but what about spiritually? The only way a woman is weaker, spiritually speaking, is in marriage. Because of her position of servitude and the wrong attitudes that can be firmly in place in people's way of thinking, she is at the mercy of her husband, and without godly love mercy can prove to be cruel in any relationship.

The Apostle Peter established both the attitude and response a husband must have toward his wife to ensure her dignity and safety within this relationship. The husband must honor her. In other words, he must prefer or exalt her to the proper place in their relationship to ensure his prayers remain effective.

All too often, a woman finds herself becoming, not only under subjection to her husband at home, but also to every man in the church. <u>There are no scriptural grounds for this practice</u> in the Body of Christ.

The Church is the bride of Christ. Each believer makes up this bride. Christ is the head and Lord of His Body. He will not take second position to the rule of man in any believer's life.

Jeremiah 17:5 and 7 warns us not to lean on the arm of the flesh in any type of dependency or reliance. To do so would put us under a curse. Blessing only comes out of trusting the Lord and putting confidence in Him.

We know from Scripture woman was made last, but we also read in the Word that women were the first ones to be used by God in many situations. Some Bible scholars maintain the first one to believe the message of redemption was Eve. The word "Eve" means the "mother of all living." Adam did not give her this name until after the fall in the Garden of Eden.[7]

Adam knew the consequence for his act of disobedience was death or separation from God. What type of life was Adam referring to in giving Eve her name—the mere physical life of mankind or the eternal life that would come through Christ?

Eve believed God when He promised redemption. This was made evident when Cain was born. According to Bushnell, the original translation of Genesis 4:1 should read, "I have gotten a man, --even 'The Coming One!'"[8]

"The Coming One" means "Jehovah." "Jehovah" in Greek means "Lord," Although Cain was not the "Promised One," Eve's belief in the "Coming One" qualified her to be a believer. John 1:12 declares, "But as many as receive

---

[7] Genesis 3:20
[8] God's Word to Women, study note 77

him, to them gave he power to become the sons of God, even to them that believer on his name."

It is interesting to note women were the first to name the Lord Jesus Christ. Eve was the first one to refer to Him as "Jehovah" or "Lord". Hannah was the first to call Him "The Anointed One" or "The Christ."[9] Mary, the mother of Christ, was the first one told to call Him "Jesus" in Luke 1:31.

Philippians 2:9-11 states this about the name of the Lord Jesus Christ,

> Wherefore, God also hath highly exalted him, and given him a name which is above every name, That at the name of Jesus every knee should bow, of things in heaven, and things in earth, and things under the earth, And that every tongue should confess that Jesus Christ is Lord, to the glory of God the Father.

We can conclude that God not only chose woman to bring forth His Son, but, from all appearances, He also ordained that they would be the first ones to declare His Son's name. Acts 4:12 summarizes the significance of this name, "Neither is there salvation in any other; for there is no other name under heaven given among men, whereby we must be saved."

This brings us to women's responses towards the Christ. Women may have been formed last, but many times they were first to perform God's work in the kingdom. Anna was a prophetess who spent forty-four years of her life in the temple. When Mary brought Jesus to the temple

---
[9] 1 Samuel 2:10

to be dedicated, Anna recognized Him to be "The Messiah" or "The Christ." Luke 2:38 tells us that she went forth and spoke to all of them there who were looking for redemption in Jerusalem. Because of her response, Anna is considered to be the <u>first</u> evangelist to the Jews.

Mary, the sister of Martha, was the <u>first</u> to anoint Jesus for His burial.[10] Jesus made this statement about her action in Matthew 26:13, "Verily I say unto you, Wherever this gospel shall be preached in the whole world, there shall also this, that this woman hath done, be told for a memorial of her."

Mary Magdalene was the <u>first</u> one to witness the empty tomb. She would also be the <u>first</u> one to proclaim Jesus' resurrection to the disciples who were in hiding. Lydia was the <u>first</u> convert in Europe. We know the <u>first</u> church in Europe met in her home in Philippi. Later, this church would be commended by Paul in his epistle to the believers of this new body.[11]

In Luke 18:14b we read this principle, "…for everyone that exalteth himself shall be abased; and he that humbleth himself shall be exalted."

As I studied how women were the first in many situations, I remembered the words of Luke 18:14. It is obvious that women have been made the tail in so many areas relating to the kingdom of God. In spite of man's rush to subject and subdue womankind, God has raised many godly women into places of greatness. These places not

---

[10] John 12:3-7
[11] Matthew 28:1-10; John 20:1-18; Acts 16:11-15, 40; Philippians 4:10-19

only reveal women quietly running the spiritual race, but they show them pressing past man-made obstacles to be all that their Lord ordained them to be. Because of their availability, they have been chosen first in many instances, therefore, exalting them in the kingdom of God.

Jesus made this statement in Matthew 19:30, "But many that are first shall be last, and the last shall be first." The meaning of this scripture has other applications than my use of it regarding women, but, nevertheless, the implications remain true.

Considering my struggle over the subject of women in God's kingdom, I had to face my own fears. Initially, I could not understand how God could put women into bondage. My overwhelming fear was that God would turn out to be the "male chauvinist" the few misconstrued, out-of-context scriptures purported Him to be. I was uneasy that, just because of something beyond my control, meaning my gender, I would be condemned to a life I could never accept in my heart.

Pushing past anxieties and risking my faith, I set out in search of truth. Truth never fails those who desire to find it. It did vindicate my scriptural perception of God. He does not "change like shifting shadows."[12] He looks at the heart and not the gender. He sits on the throne and uses what vessel He will. He exalts those who are abased.

The result of my search for truth confirmed what I had suspected all along. God does not have favorites. I am now stronger in my belief. My discouragement has turned into

---

[12] James 1:17

joy, my oppression into liberty, and my adversity into victory. Through it all, I gained insight into my true identity in the kingdom of God. I do not stand before God as a "woman," but as "His child." I do not have to accept the crumbs of man when my Lord has offered me a full meal—for He is the Bread of Life and the Giver of Living Water.

I have learned it is okay to be last, for it is in one's weakness that God's greatness is learned. It is because of need that many accept God's invitation to sup with Him. It is in the darkest of times of such need that some will come out with a greater revelation of Jesus. It is in lack that others learn contentment in Christ

In my struggle, I have learned it is not ministry that verifies spiritual success. Spiritual success is grasped when one learns to lose in order to gain. As believers, we must all forsake our self-importance and be willing to lose our identity in this world in order to gain Christ. After all, Christ is our reward and inheritance. If we have Christ, we have it all.

Now I can truly say, "Thank you God, for making me last."

10

CAN WOMEN BE ENTRUSTED?

We have already discussed how God chooses the most unlikely vessels to use for His glory. His decision is not based on sex, as many have tried to prove by using certain passages of scripture. The major issue in the kingdom is quite simple; what vessel can God entrust with his work?

Throughout scripture, we see God commending women. We already know God used a virgin by the name of Mary to bring forth His Son. In Judges 4-5, God entrusted the prophetess, Deborah, to lead the armies of Israel into a victorious battle. In the book of Esther, we read of God's miraculous intervention to save the nation of Israel when He moved Mordecai's niece, Esther, into a position of intercession with the king on behalf of His people.

Although a source of much controversy in the Church, Rebekah took action on what God revealed to her about her two sons. Bear in mind that Isaac dealt in the realm of both the material world and the tradition in determining which son would inherit the promise. Rebekah saw beyond to God's plan. Her intervention may be classified as deceptive, but, nevertheless, it was a fulfillment of God's will.[1]

In Judges 13:3, we read of the angel first appearing to Samson's mother to declare his conception. In 1 Samuel 1:26-28, we see how it was Hannah who dedicated Samuel to the Lord. It was the harlot, Rahab, who hid the two spies from Israel's enemies in Jericho. A Moabite woman named Ruth left home and family to follow her mother-in-law to her homeland, Israel. Both of these pagan ladies are named in the lineage of Jesus.[2]

Scripturally, we see women being used in every facet in the kingdom of God. Like Deborah, some were leaders of God's people. In the New Testament, Phoebe would be Deborah's counterpart. Once again, we are reminded that this godly woman served in the position of a deacon. There was also Junia. According to the spelling of the name, it points to a woman who was noted among the apostles.[3]

Women were also used in temple work. Exodus 38:8 and 1 Samuel 2:22 imply women served in the tabernacle at stated intervals, as did the priests. Numbers 6:2 tells us that women could be Nazarites. Exodus 38:8 states, "And he made the laver of brass, and the foot of it of brass, of the looking glasses of the women assembling, which assembled at the door of the tabernacle of the congregation."

---

[1] Genesis 25:22-23
[2] Joshua 2, Ruth 1; Matthew 1:5
[3] Difficult Sayings (article)

Ruth Specter Lascelle made this comment about Exodus 38:8, "In typology the Laver represents the WORD OF GOD. The looking-glasses were made of highly polished brass (copper) into which the women would look to see a reflection of themselves. The Word of God is like a mirror which reflects what we look like and it tells of a remedy whereby we can be cleansed. These looking-glasses were donated by the Jewish women for the building of the Laver."

In the New Testament, the believer serves as the temple of the Holy Spirit. The Apostle Paul encouraged the single women to remain so and consecrate themselves totally to God and His work.[4] 1 Peter 2:5 says, "Ye also, as lively stones, are built up a spiritual house, and holy priesthood, to offer up spiritual sacrifices, acceptable to God by Jesus Christ."

We can clearly see that women's roles have not varied in either of the testaments. Women have been placed in spiritual leadership positions. For instance, Moses' sister, Miriam, was a prophetess. She was accredited with leading the children of Israel, along with Moses and Aaron through the wilderness.[5]

The priests went to the prophetess, Huldah, to find out the mind of the Lord in 2 Kings 22:14-20. The word "prophecy" is described by Paul in 1 Corinthians 14:3 in this manner: "But he that prophesieth speaketh unto men to edification, and exhortation and comfort."

---

[4] 1 Corinthians 6:19-20; 7:25-26, 34-35
[5] Exodus 15:20-21; Micah 6:4

Pastor W. L. Myers explained in his book, *Does God Call Women to Preach?*, that the meaning of prophecy in 1 Corinthians 14:3 can be ascribed to the definition of preaching as well. Preaching is more than proclaiming; it edifies, exhorts, and comforts.

Acts 21:8-9 tells us,

> And the next day we that were of Paul's company departed, and came unto Caesarea; and we entered into the house of Philip, the evangelist, who was one of the seven, and abode with him. And the same man had four daughters, virgins, who did prophesy.

According to historical information, these four women evangelized throughout the then known world. They preached in parks, in public buildings, and in halls.[6] This should not surprise us since a Christian's commission is to preach the good news to all creation.[7]

Obviously, preaching is not limited to men. Every time a woman proclaims Christ, she is fulfilling her commission. We know Anna and Mary Magdalene were evangelists, but so was the woman at the well. While Jesus was talking to His disciples about the harvest field, the Samaritan woman was sharing Christ with the men of the city.[8]

According to archaeological findings, etchings and paintings have been found on the walls of catacombs depicting women preaching and serving communion.[9] Acts

---

[6] Women In Today's Church, page 20
[7] Mark 16:15
[8] John 4:28-29
[9] Women In Today's Church, page 29

1:14 tells us that women were part of the group waiting to be endued with power from above.[10] Therefore, these women had to be declaring the Gospel along with the men.

Some would contend that the commission of proclaiming the Gospel is different from the position of being a preacher. I realize there is a position of shepherd or pastor in the church, but there is no scriptural reference to stipulate this position is limited to a man. Recent history even proves differently when you consider the staggering work done by women on the mission field.

Again, we must refer back to the definition of prophecy. Prophecy involves forth-telling, expounding scripture for the purpose of instruction. The Apostle Paul made this statement in 1 Corinthians 14:1, "Follow after charity, and desire spiritual gifts, but rather that ye may prophesy." According to Paul, prophecy was beneficial for the building up of the Church. He desired that all would have this gift.

Preaching by women can be found in the Old Testament. Psalm 68:11 says, "The Lord gave the word; great was the company of those who published it." Lascelle gives this insight into this Scripture,

> The word "company" is in the feminine gender. The words of action (i.e. "proclaimed" or "published") telling what this feminine "company" is doing, is also in the feminine gender, since this is the proper Hebrew grammar. The word "company" implies that it is an army that assembles by troops. These words, "assembling" and "assembled" (KJV)

---
[10] Luke 24:49

in Exodus 38:8 along with the word "company" in Psalm 68:11 tells that the Lord gave the WORD (the Laver) and there was a feminine army who published or PREACHED it! The R.V. gives it as "The Lord giveth the Word. The WOMEN that publish the tidings are a great host.

Godly women comprise a powerful army in God. They have led God's people in various ways. They have been pillars in the Church. They faithfully served alongside the Apostle Paul in the harvest field. We see Paul commending some of these women for their commitment to the Gospel in Romans 16:3, 6 & 12.

Paul referred to Priscilla as a fellow worker. According to *Vine's Expository Dictionary of Biblical Words*, "fellow workers" implies equality in importance and position. He acknowledged Mary, Tryphena, Tryphosa, and Persis' hard work in the Lord. In Romans 16:13, the Apostle Paul sent a greeting to Rufus and his mother whom Paul also claimed to be his mother. Was Rufus' mother Paul's biological mother or did he consider her to be his spiritual mother?

Bible scholars note that Priscilla's name was used before her husband's name in a couple Scriptures such as Acts 18:18 and Romans 16:3. According to the culture of that time, putting Priscilla's name first indicated leadership or importance in that particular reference. Based on my various studies, she appears to be the dominant minister and teacher in this husband-and-wife team. We know

Priscilla played a major role in instructing Apollo.[11] Many believe she was the believing wife Paul made reference to in 1 Corinthians 9:5 (Refer to 1 Corinthians 16:19). According to Romans 16:3, she had risked her life for Paul and other believers.

This brings me to the unrealistic mindset some church leaders have adopted towards women holding leadership positions in the Church. Quick to accept women as missionaries in foreign countries, some of these same leaders hypocritically deny these same women the position and recognition in the Church in America.

These women have served as apostles, prophets, evangelists, pastors, and teachers on the mission field. They have laid down their lives for the Gospel; yet, they still cannot be entrusted with leadership positions in the Church. It appears as if some men are trying to maintain their comfortable positions behind the pulpit in the name of scriptural instruction, while ignoring the price their female counterparts have had to pay to serve on the mission field.

In fact, the latest ratio of women to men in the mission field is sixteen women to one man. Certain men can go around advocating why women must come into bondage to their way of thinking because of a few Scriptures, but statistics reveal that it is the women that continue to work in the harvest field. Where would the souls be today that have been affected by the devotion of women if those women would have allowed themselves to be silenced by

---

[11] Acts 18:18-19, 24-26

a few misused Scriptures, rather than faithfully adhered to their high calling in Christ?

One must wonder what happened from the time women of the new Church were used in a powerful way to the present time. Obviously, women have been demoted to the position of silent, mindless zombies in the scheme of things, who have no other option but to become subservient to all of man's conclusions and whims. Some believe it had to do with the pressures of what would be more accepted by the culture and the societal values within the last part of the first century of the new Church. These pressures resulted in women's roles being minimized.[12] Apparently, in the attempt to justify this unfounded demotion, Scriptures were either adjusted in their presentation or added.

Regardless of this mindset, the Word establishes the truth about women. God has entrusted women with much. They were in the upper room at Pentecost and named among those of "whom the world was not worthy" in Hebrews 11. Their actions were upheld by the Lord to serve as a memorial and example to others. They preached, held leadership positions, and worked hard for the kingdom of God. They even suffered and died for the sake of their Lord and the furtherance of the kingdom of God.

Here is a simple question, If God entrusted women with leadership in the kingdom of God, then who is mere man within his religious organization, to declare certain areas

---

[12] Difficult Sayings (article)

off limits to them? Whose kingdom is being "protected" from the influence of women—God's kingdom or man's?

11

LET MY HANDMAIDENS GO!

I have learned true service to God hinges on having the liberty to be what God desires us to be. In Exodus, God made this request of Pharaoh, "Let my people go." The reason that Pharaoh had to let the people go was so that they could serve and worship God.[1]

Humankind has been formed by God to worship and be in fellowship with Him. It is only in a growing relationship with God that we, as believers, will glorify Him. However, it takes the liberty of the Spirit to worship God in spirit and truth. It is truth that makes us free to discover the reality of our Lord and Savior, and to be all that He desires us to be in His kingdom.[2]

People who are in bondage cannot be available to God. They are too busy striving to serve two masters. Divided loyalties bring nothing but frustration and double-

---

[1] Exodus 7:16; 8:20; 9:1, 13
[2] John 4:24; 8:32-36; 2 Corinthians 3:17

mindedness that will always lead to spiritual, mental, and emotional instability.[3]

God was clearly asking Pharaoh to let His people go to worship Him. This worship involved offering sacrifices. Romans 12:1 instructs us to offer our bodies as a living sacrifice, which is our reasonable service. This sacrifice points to one consecrating their life wholly to the Lord.

Christians must have liberty in the Spirit in order to present their bodies as a living sacrifice. This sacrifice is necessary to ensure a life that will do that which is good, acceptable, and according to God's perfect will.[4].

Jesus made this statement in Matthew 12:48b-50 about who was part of the family of God, "...Who is my mother? And who are my brethren? And he stretched forth his hand toward his disciples, and said, Behold my mother and my brethren! For whosoever shall do the will of my Father, who is in heaven, the same is my brother, and sister, and mother."

Jesus made no distinction of gender when He made reference to the family of God. He revealed the simple ingredient to be a part of His family—doing the will of the Father.

Who determines the will of the Father? Romans 11:33-34 informs us that the riches of the wisdom and knowledge of God are unsearchable. There is no way mere man can know the mind of the Lord for himself or others. It is only by the Holy Spirit that we can discover, know, and

---

[3] James 1:8
[4] Romans 12:2

experience the depth of God and come to terms with what is His personal will for our lives.

Many times, man has put God in a box. He has tried to confine God's ways to fit his understanding and pride. But God's ways and thoughts are higher than ours. They are righteous and perfect; therefore, there is no inconsistency in His dealings with mankind.[5]

How can man ensure he is lining up with the ways of God? Proverbs 4:7 instructs us to get wisdom, no matter how much it might cost us. Psalm 111:10 tells us the fear of the Lord is the beginning of wisdom. Ecclesiastes 12:13 summarizes the whole duty of man as fearing God and keeping His commandments. Philippians 2:12 commands us to work out our salvation in fear and trembling.

Although Proverbs 31 is often quoted to show woman how she is to act, the secret behind all godly women is revealed in Proverbs 31:30, "Favor is deceitful, and beauty is vain, but a woman who feareth the LORD, she shall be praised." The fear of the Lord is an awesome reverence towards God. This reverence will hate evil, serve as one's confidence towards God, and become a fountain of life.[6]

Fear of God is also vital if one is to see the importance of doing it God's way. Man is quick to lose sight of the holiness of his God. It is easy for man to take lightly the things of God. However, when one has the fear of the Lord, they keep the reality of God's righteousness before their eyes.

---

[5] Psalm 18:30; Isaiah 55:8-9
[6] Proverbs 8:13; 14:26-27

Another aspect of the Christian life is love or charity. Love is the heartbeat of Christianity. It is a commitment to be <u>right</u> before God and to do <u>right</u> by those around us. This love is patient and kind. It is not envious, proud, or rude. It is not selfish; therefore, it does not demand its own way. It is meek (teachable) in nature, pursues peace, desires truth, and remains faithful. It is benevolent, which means it will possess good will and kindness.[7]

This love must be evident in everyone who claims to be a Christian. It must exist between believers and between husbands and wives. It results in submission, and will always prefer others over self. It is for this reason, love ultimately serves as the test of true Christianity.[8]

God's love is sacrificial. It will deny self and exalt the needs of others. It will not value the ways of man, but seeks to please God. It does not desire to control. Rather it desires to see one discover their real potential in God. It does not rejoice in the iniquity of bondage, but in truth reigning in a situation. It is real and persevering. Above all else, it will bring glory to God.[9]

Satan hates God and His people. One of his greatest devices is bondage. He does not care how he secures the captivity of people, whether he uses the different fears that plague us or the sin that can so easily beset us. He does not care if he uses lies, adjusts the Word, man's religion, or the wickedness of others, he wants people to be in bondage to his ways of death and destruction.

---

[7] 1 Corinthians 7:3; 13; 1 John 3:10
[8] 1 John 3:14-15
[9] John 3:16; 13:34-35; 1 Corinthians 13:6-7; 1 John 3:16

Such bondage implies control and inferiority. Inferiority among humanity is a product of an outward judgment based on man's standards. Such judgment proves to be unmerciful. It is contrary to the very nature of God's love, mercy, compassion, and grace.[10]

Bondage destroys not only its victims, but also those who are part of the enslaving process. Individuals who enslave others will ultimately find themselves in bondage themselves. Galatians 6:7-8 confirms this principle, "Be not deceived, God is not mocked, for whatsoever a man soweth, that shall he also reap. For he that soweth to his flesh shall of the flesh reap corruption; but he that soweth to the Spirit shall of the Spirit reap life everlasting."

Liberty is associated with the Spirit of God, and bondage with the flesh of man. It is clear that the Holy Spirit must be evident in our attitudes, ways, and practices if we are going to reap eternal value. In Exodus 10:7-11 we read that Pharaoh agreed to allow the men to go worship God, but not the women or the children. Moses refused to accept his stipulation. God's demand remained the same, "Let <u>my people</u> go . . ."

If Christian women are in bondage in any way, God's command is the same for today as it was during Moses' day. He wants those who are Pharaohs in heart to let His handmaidens go to worship Him! Although they came out of the side of man, they came from the heart of God. They do not belong to man. They are not here to serve man's

---

[10] John 8:44; Romans 6:6-7; 2 Timothy 1:7; 2:26; Hebrews 12:1
James 2:13

whims. They are here to bring glory to their Creator in service to their family.

As long as women are in bondage to man's religious standards, the Church remains in captivity, for when one member suffers, the whole body suffers.[11] There is nothing more heart wrenching than to watch an individual who desires liberty in God be put down in the name of Christ because of physical traits (gender) the person had no power in determining.

This captivity will benefit no one but the kingdom of darkness. It will keep women who have the call of God and the desire, devotion, and ability to serve Him from making a vital difference in the Church, as well as in the lives of those who live in darkness.

Like Barak, who submitted to the leadership of Deborah, it is a show of faith to let God use the vessel He chooses. Although Deborah helped lead the army, Barak was still accredited with conquering kingdoms. His name is listed with the great heroes of the faith in Hebrews 11. After all, true faith is letting God be God. If God chooses woman to lead, so be it. Great men of faith will always submit, for there is only one correct goal in the kingdom of God—to glorify God and to build up His people.

Although the entire Church today does not promote the bondage that enslaves women, those who do are adhering to Satan's rules. As long as they insist on maintaining this bondage, the Church is being held in a cage. Like Israel, true worship cannot occur until <u>all of God's people are set</u>

---

[11] 1 Corinthians 12:26

<u>free to present themselves as living sacrifices for His glory</u>. Without humility and worship, there is no revival. If there is no revival, the demons dance with joy because they are gaining ground.

The kingdom of God is not a matter of competition. If there is a job to do, who cares what type of vessel is used as long as the job gets done for the glory of God and the benefit of His kingdom? Myers made this statement in his book *Does God Call Women to Preach*?

> Some preachers remind me of Joshua, when he came running in, eyes blared, nostrils dilated crying, 'My Lord, Eldad and Medad do prophesy in the camp.' But Moses said, 'Son, I wish <u>all</u> God's people were prophets.' (Numbers 11:28, 29). Moses was not envious. He was not afraid the ladies would root him out of his pulpit. Neither am I.

Church, what will it be? Liberty for all or bondage? There is no middle ground. Liberty must happen on an individual level before it can occur collectively. It begins with the heart, invades the attitude, and results in submission, not only to God, but also to each other in brotherly love.

If you are a woman who feels the oppression of religious bondage, take heart! Like Israel, God will intercede on your behalf and force the issue of liberty for you. He provided the means by which Pharaoh would let His people go. The means was the Passover Lamb.

Women, you have a Passover Lamb. His name is Jesus Christ. All you have to do is present yourself to Him as a living sacrifice. Once you come under His reign, He will fight for you. In the end, you will be able to sing a song of victory like the people of Israel in Exodus 15:1-3, 11, 13, 17-18,

> I will sing unto the LORD, for he hath triumphed gloriously...The Lord is my strength and song, and he is become my salvation; he is my God, and I will prepare him an habitation; my father's God, and I will exalt him. The LORD is a man of war; the LORD is his name...Who is like unto thee, O LORD, among the gods? Who is like thee, glorious in holiness, fearful in praises, doing wonders?...Thou in thy mercy hast led forth the people whom thou hast redeemed; thou has guided them in thy strength unto thy holy habitation...Thou shalt bring them in, and plant them in the mountain of thine inheritance, in the place, O LORD, which thou has made for thee to dwell in, in the sanctuary, O Lord, which thy hands have established. The LORD shall reign forever and ever.

12

A FINAL THOUGHT

When reading the prophet Jeremiah, I came to a couple of very interesting scriptures,

> For since I spake, I cried out, I cried violence and spoil; because the word of the LORD was made a reproach unto me, and a derision, daily. Then I said, I will not make mention of him, nor speak any more in his name. But his word was in mine heart as a burning fire shut up in my bones, and I was weary with forbearing, and I could not stay (Jeremiah 20:8-9).

Jeremiah suffered much persecution and rejection from the people of Israel. He was speaking the truth, but they did not want to hear it. They were resting on their laurels as descendants of Abraham and not testing or discerning whether their God was pleased with their attitudes and ways. They wanted their ears tickled by false prophets and not their spirit awakened to sin, their souls brought low, and their hearts broken over their sin. They needed to truly repent but they did not want to wear sackcloth that made them uncomfortable in their sin and pour ashes of sorrow upon their head showing loss, despair, and misery because not all was well in their relationship with God.

The Jewish people were standing on a false foundation, hiding behind a false hope and preferring delusion rather than the truth. In their delusion they could operate in wishful thinking that they had enough piousness to appear righteous, and that their God would certainly not allow them to be judged by pagan nations because they were His chosen people through Abraham.

It was clear that Jeremiah's decision to give up speaking what God had laid on his heart, indicated that he had become weary with contending with stiff-necked people. He was contending for souls but they would have none of it, and they did all they could to silence him. He was about ready to give them their wish except for one thing; he could not deny the burning of God's words in his heart. He needed to speak them or be consumed by them.

I want to encourage any servant of God to not consider how man is looking at you or treating you; rather, keep your eyes on Your Lord. It does not matter that we please man in his fickle state in order to get along; rather, we must please God if we are going to know the liberation of His truth and the freedom and power of His Spirit to reach our high calling. Nothing happens outside of the Lord's control and He knows how to work all things for your good and His glory.

When I started this journey to come to my place in God's kingdom I came up against the conventional, the acceptable, and the controllable. I wrestled with my place because I did not fit in man's design when it came to his religious ways and practices. As I have already shared, I either had to ignore, snuff out, or douse what started as a small flame but was growing into a burning passion.

It is because of the burning passion you realize that to deny its presence in your being will mean the end of you because it is more powerful than all the other senses you have felt. At that point you are willing to let the chips fall where they may because there is nothing that is going to make sense to you from that point on. You are in fact desperate enough to go against any grain or flow to bring contentment to your soul and be at peace with God.

It is in this state, you are not willing to put God in a box so you can get along with others, and on the other hand, you are not willing to be put in a box so that you fit in. You can't or won't settle for being greatly oppressed and miserable because you are missing the mark of God's high calling on your life. You must remember that anything that is of, or from, God will always prove to be higher and more excellent than you can imagine.

I realize that the hindrances, rejection, and battles I have faced due to my place and calling in God's kingdom was minor to what so many saints, both men and women, have faced before me. However, I also realize that God used it all to forge me and bring out my calling and giftings, but I had to walk through the challenges, face the failures, endure the rejection, and hold to the truth through the battles.

Like Jeremiah, during some of the most difficult times of my walk, I have thought about giving up and trying to find some normalcy that I had left behind. I found myself falling into a pit of despair due to the inner struggle of what I considered to be my own failures in ministry. In this state of confusion, I questioned if I was missing the mark that God had put on my heart because I was unknowingly demanding my way, even though I was aware of my reluctance in the past to pursue my calling and the challenging obstacles of the present that sometimes brought me to anguish.

As a result, in our pathetic humanity we can become like Peter in John 21, and go back to fishing, but every such notion should remind us at such times that he ended up empty handed and had to come back to Jesus and once again declare his love for Him.

In one incident I saw myself spiritually sitting in the middle of the road when the Lord gave me a choice. I could turn aside and go to the plush valleys like Lot did where future judgment was pending, or I could go back to the ovens in Daniel 3 with Shadrach, Meshach, and Abednego to walk with the Son of God. I chose the latter.

To turn back is to betray my Lord. It is to act as if He, in some, way failed me, forsook me, or let the wolves devour my calling. To surrender when God has given me everything I need of to stand in His strength, withstand in His power, and to continue to stand is contemptuous. It reveals that I have chosen unbelief rather than faith and obedience.

In my journey I have met both men and women that have a calling but find that their faith towards God is being tested because it is contrary to the religious current of the age. The reasons for, or the excuses behind such testing, really do not matter. What matters is that God will always have a remnant that will not fit, will not play in some religious sandbox with others, and will not go along with the crowd, religious or not.

They will not only be the "odd man or woman out" of the acceptable scheme of things, but they will rub the nominal wrong, shake the acceptable, and collide with the understandable. As Hebrews 11 pointed out about those who walked by faith, they knew the bitterness of trials, losses, and rejection, causing them to often stand alone and wander in the barren desert of the world.

These individuals of faith past and present are not deterred by any of it because they are looking beyond this world to a greater glory. They, in fact, are looking for a better resurrection, and when it is all said and done, that which is of this world, no matter how religious and pious it might be, will prove it was not even worthy to witness these individuals' abiding faith towards and in their Lord God Almighty.

BIBLIOGRAPHY

Strong's Exhaustive Concordance of the Bible; James Strong, © 1986 assigned to World Bible Publishers, Inc

Webster's New Collegiate Dictionary; © 1976 by G. & C. Merriam Co.

Vine's Expository Dictionary of Biblical Words; © 1985 by Thomas Nelson, Inc., Publishers

A Dwelling Place For God; by Ruth Specter Lascelle; © 1990 by Hyman Israel Specter, Van Nuys CA.

Women In Today's Church; George Watkins; ©1984

The Laver (Article); Ruth Specter Lascelle

Jewish Faith and the New Covenant; Ruth Specter Lascelle © 1980

When Saints Go Marching; Ethel Ruff; 1957

Does God Call Women To Preach?; Rev. W. L. Myers; 1948

God's Word to Women (1923) 100 Bible Studies by Katharine C. Bushnell

Internet Articles:

Today's Word; Skip Moen, At Gods Table. com. ©2003

"Difficult Sayings" Jonathan Went; © 2002-2005; http://www.studylight.org/col/ds/

Other books by Rayola Kelley:

Hidden Manna (Original)
Battle for the Soul
Stories of the Heart
Transforming Love & Beyond
The Great Debate
The Journey of a Lifetime (Author's Autobiography)
Post to Post: (1) Establishing the Way
Post to Post: (2) Walking in the Way
Post to Post: (3) Meditations Along the Way
Post to Post: (4) Inspirations Along the Way
Post to Post: (5) Collecting Gems Along the Way

Volume One: Establishing Our Life in Christ
My Words are Spirit and Life
The Anatomy of Sin
The Principles of the Abundant Life
The Place of Covenant
*Unmasking the Cult Mentality

Volume Two: Putting on the Life of Christ
He Actually Thought it Not Robbery
Revelation of the Cross
*In Search of Real Faith
Think on These Things
Follow the Pattern

Volume Three: Developing a Godly Environment
Godly Discipline
Prayer and Worship
Don't Touch That Dial
Face of Thankfulness
ABC's of Christianity

Volume Four: Issues of the Heart
*Hidden Manna (Revised)
Bring Down the Sacred Cows
The Manual for the Single Christian Life
Parents are People Too

Volume Five: Challenging the Christian Life
The Issues of Life
Presentation of the Gospel
*For the Purpose of Edification
Whatever Happened to the Church?
*Women's Place in the Kingdom of God

Volume Six: Developing Our Christian Life
The Many Faces of Christianity
*Possessing Our Souls
Experiencing the Christian Life
The Power of Our Testimonies
*The Victorious Journey

Devotions
Devotions of the Heart: Books One and Two
Daily Food for the Soul: Books One and Two

Gentle Shepherd Ministries Devotion Series:
Being a Child of God
Disciplining the Strength of our Youth
Coming to Full Age

Nugget Books:
Nuggets From Heaven
More Nuggets From Heaven
Heavenly Gems
More Heavenly Gems
Heavenly Treasures
More Heavenly Treasures

Gentle Shepherd Ministries Series:

The Christian Life Series
What Matter Is This?
The Challenge of It
The Reality of It

The Leadership Series
Overcoming
A Matter of Authority and Power
The Dynamics of True Leadership

Books By:
Jeannette Haley

Books co-authored with Rayola Kelley:
Hidden Manna (original)
The Many Faces of Christianity (Volume 6)
Post to Post 3: Meditations Along the Way
Post to Post 4: Inspirations Along the Way
Post to Post 5: Collecting Gems Along the Way

Other Books:
Rose of Light, Thorn of Darkness
Interview In Hell}
Interview On Earth}
(Both Interview Books are now in one book
Angelus Assignments)
The Pig and I
Reflections of Wonder (Devotional)

Children's Books:
Little Stories for Little People
Traveler's Tales
The Adventures of Zack and Mira
The Adventures of Paul and Dana
(A House on the Beach)
The Monster of Mystery Valley

*Books that have been separated from the volumes and are now available under their own titles.

www.ingramcontent.com/pod-product-compliance
Lightning Source LLC
Chambersburg PA
CBHW070502100426
42743CB00010B/1725